Scripture Discussion Commentary 11

SCRIPTURE DISCUSSION COMMENTARY 11

Series editor: Laurence Bright

Paul II

1 Corinthians *Laurence Bright*
2 Corinthians *Henry Wansbrough*
Philippians *Jerome Murphy-O'Connor*
Colossians *Jerome Murphy-O'Connor*
Philemon *Laurence Bright*

ACTA Foundation
Adult Catechetical Teaching Aids
Chicago, Illinois

First published 1971
ACTA Foundation (Adult Catechetical Teaching Aids),
4848 N. Clark Street, Chicago, Illinois 60640
© 1971, Laurence Bright, Henry Wansbrough, Jerome Murphy-O'Connor
Nihil obstat: John M. T. Barton STD LSS *Censor*
Imprimatur: + Victor Guazzelli *Vicar General*
Westminster, 15th July 1971

2548

Library of Congress number 71–173033

SBN 0 87946 010 5

Made and printed in Great Britain by
William Clowes & Sons, Limited
London, Beccles and Colchester

Contents

General Introduction

General Introduction

A few of the individual units which make up this series of biblical commentaries have already proved their worth issued as separate booklets. Together with many others they are now grouped together in a set of twelve volumes covering almost all the books of the old and new testaments—a few have been omitted as unsuitable to the general purpose of the series.

That purpose is primarily to promote discussion. This is how these commentaries differ from the others that exist. They do not cover all that could be said about the biblical text, but concentrate on the features most likely to get lively conversation going—those, for instance, with special relevance for later developments of thought, or for life in the church and world of today. For this reason passages of narrative are punctuated by sets of questions designed to get a group talking, though the text of scripture, helped by the remarks of the commentator, should have already done just that.

For the text is what matters. Individuals getting ready for a meeting, the group itself as it meets, should always have the bible centrally present, and use the commentary only as a tool. The bibliographies will help those wishing to dig deeper.

What kinds of group can work in this way? Absolutely

any. The bible has the reputation of being difficult, and
in some respects it is, but practice quickly clears up a lot
of initial obstacles. So parish groups of any kind can and
should be working on it. The groups needn't necessarily
already exist, it is enough to have a few like-minded
friends and to care sufficiently about finding out what the
bible means. Nor need they be very large; one family
could be quite enough. High schools (particularly in the
senior year), colleges and universities are also obvious
places for groups to form. If possible they should everywhere be ecumenical in composition: though all the
authors are Roman catholics, there is nothing sectarian
in their approach.

In each volume there are two to four, or occasionally
more, studies of related biblical books. Each one is self-
contained; it is neither necessary nor desirable to start at
the beginning and plough steadily through. Take up,
each time, what most interests you—there is very little in
scripture that is actually dull! Since the commentaries
are by different authors, you will discover differences of
outlook, in itself a matter for discussion. Above all, remember that getting the right general approach to reading the bible is more important than answering any
particular question about the text—and that this approach
only comes with practice.

LAURENCE BRIGHT

1 Corinthians

Laurence Bright

Introduction

St Paul and 1 Corinthians

Paul's letters are a good deal easier for us to understand than any of the gospels. English-speaking catholics may find this rather odd; part of the myth they believe in is that the gospels are the plain, straightforward accounts of the life of Jesus, whereas Paul represents a slightly perverse attempt to introduce a complexity we could well have done without. It comes as rather a shock to realise that all the genuine pauline epistles, even Colossians, may well have been completed before the first gospel appeared. Paul's thought is undeniably profound, yet his letters were written to ordinary christians like ourselves—the same men and women who listened to the preaching out of which the gospels themselves grew. The difficulty of the epistles is due partly to a theological idiom with which we are unfamiliar (especially in its use of the old testament), partly to their 'occasional' nature in contexts we cannot always reconstruct, partly to Paul's own impetuous character; all things which time and patience will sort out. But there is far less merely implicit statement whose meaning we pass over because it is given through the symbolism of action and situation, far less allusiveness—altogether far less stuff that once could be taken for granted but no longer means a thing—than in the earliest gospel. Paul raises fewer problems of form-criticism; ie, there isn't the absolute need, as with the gospels, first of all to place each narrative in its context. These are not matters which a reader who wishes to enter into the gospel (except at a superficial level) can afford to pass over, but they are much less basic to the understanding of Paul. Of course Paul and gospel alike also raise problems in plenty for the scholar—problems of text and dating and authenticity; but these can be safely left to those who enjoy them.

1 Corinthians strikingly shows many aspects of Paul's thought. Like Romans, it represents the mind of Paul at the central period of his development, yet it is less solemn than Romans. It gives us plenty of theological ideas to work with, yet they are manageable because they grow readily out of the practical situation with which Paul has to deal. No one could even begin to mistake it for a formal treatise; indeed, it often disconcerts us with a mass of detail that at first seems quite irrelevant to our concerns. The best background account is Acts—all of it if possible, but certainly Chapter 18. Acts, it is true, was written thirty or more years later, and is essentially a theological account, less reliable for historical detail than the occasional remarks we get in Paul's own letters. But very often Acts is all we have to go on. There we see Paul on his missionary journeys, penetrating further and further into Greece, and reaching Corinth about AD 50, some twenty years after the resurrection had taken place. As usual he went to the Jewish synagogue, where as a rabbi he had the right to preach, and as usual his exposition of the new way of christianity caused a row, so that he was forced to break with the synagogue and set up a separate christian assembly, which would in the main have been

made up of Jewish converts (including the ruler of the synagogue) and of gentiles who had previously accepted judaism in whole or part. Corinth was a great city and notorious for bad morals, so it is not surprising that when Paul moved on, after a year and a half there, troubles arose over both moral and doctrinal matters and caused him to write various letters, two of which survive. 1 Corinthians was probably written in AD 55 and from Ephesus in Asia Minor.

Book list

1. *Jerusalem Bible.* The introduction and notes provide a useful commentary which is always worth consulting, and there is a useful index of theological themes.

2. *Peake's Commentary.* Probably the best modern single volume commentary in English for the non-specialist. 1 Corinthians is on pp 954–66, sound but a little dull.

3. *Introduction to the New Testament* Robert and Feuillet, 423–33. A useful account of the epistle by French Roman catholic scholars.

4. *Le Christ*⎱ *dans la théologie de St Paul,* L. Cerfaux.
   L'Eglise ⎰
These are standard works to consult; they have been translated, but not very satisfactorily.

5. *Clarendon commentary on 1 Corinthians.*

6. *The Letters to the Corinthians* William Barclay. A simple commentary by an evangelical christian.

7. *The Corinthian Mirror* J. Blenkinsopp deals with some basic themes.

1

Divisions in the church
1 Cor 1:1–2:5

1 Cor 1:1–8

Paul is going to deal with divisions, so he begins by talking of the unity of the church as a whole: local church
related to universal church. All christians, he says, are
united in their confession that Christ is Lord (1:2). This
means that when God raised Jesus from death he gave
him rule, lordship, over the church, and indeed over all
creation. (Christ's rule as Lord is often spoken of in Acts,
eg 2:36; for a developed view see Col 1:15–20.) This
confession of faith in the name ('name' is the equivalent
of 'person' in semitic thought) of Jesus opens a man to
the gift of the Spirit, makes him holy (each christian is
called a 'saint', 1:2), enriched with special gifts (1:4–7).
Yet Paul sets these ideas, familiar enough to us, in a context that is less common, and which we shall have to take
account of in this letter. He speaks of the 'revealing of
our Lord' (1:8). Such ideas are usually called 'eschatological' (*eschata*, 'last things'), and refer to the central belief of christians that Christ will come (we would now
say 'come back', speak of a second coming) to end the
'present age'. This sense was far more vivid to the early
christians (their repeated phrase, probably liturgical,
seems to have been *Maranatha*, 'come Lord'; cf 16:22),
and colours all their moral teaching, for instance. This

7

'day of Yahweh', spoken of so often by the prophets as a judgement on Israel and mankind, is now seen as the 'day of the Lord Jesus' (1:8) and has, they recognised, already broken into our world with the resurrection and the sending of the Spirit. The 'age to come' (kingdom of God) has begun in this world, the decisive victory over evil powers been won (cf Col 2:9–15), yet the 'present age' still lingers on, and our task is to carry the victory into the whole of creation until Christ is truly 'all in all' (Eph 1:23). This is why the period of the church is so frequently seen in the new testament as temporary, the presence of the Spirit called only 'first-fruits' and 'pledge' of yet more to come. It is not an attitude easy to recover, yet we shall be missing a great deal if we forget it. Needless to say it has little relationship to the 'other-worldly' views of over-spiritualised modern versions of christianity.

1. What does Paul mean by 'enriched in him with all speech and knowledge'? How is christianity to fill our lives?

2. What do we understand by 'the day of our Lord Jesus Christ'? Ought we to have more sense of its imminence, if we are to avoid complacency? If so, how?

1 Cor 1:9–16

Paul now tackles the problem of divisions in the church at Corinth. It looks as if other christian missionaries besides him had instructed and baptised them, and that they had come to feel that they belonged to their sponsor's 'party', as one might in a club. Paul's answer, again, is that there is only one sponsor, Christ—other men are merely his instruments. God has called them 'into Christ's fellowship' (1:9). *Into* has a special force here; we are firmly joined to him, and thus to one another, making up a 'fellowship'. Paul is always trying to express in different ways this sense in which the community really is Christ, yet distinct: many, yet one. Later we shall see images like 'body', 'temple', 'bride' coming up. Here he says simply 'is Christ divided?' (1:13). He means the church, but he says Christ. (This is our question too, on a far greater scale.)

Paul puts the same point in two other ways in 1:13. No party-leader could replace Christ: whatever Paul or anyone else does he can do only because Christ has already done everything. Here again there is a tension that is not easy to hold properly in balance. All has been done for us—God's grace is sovereign: yet, granted that, we can cooperate with God in Christ. Paul isn't crucified for us, yet he is a true instrument of God to bring the effects of that action to us by word and sacrament. There is but one mediator, yet each one of us in and with him mediates truth and love to our fellow-men. We ought to ask ourselves how far we hold this balance: do we place too much emphasis on 'faith' or 'works'? Again Paul asks how anyone could be baptised into any other 'name' than Christ's (1:13). For it is his death and risen life we are to share (Rom 6:1-11). So there is only one baptism, christian baptism. We must realise the importance of sharing something absolutely, before being divided by expressing the one faith (as we must) according to our varying traditions.

1. Do we have to admit that for us too Christ is divided? Or is the sense in which we are one in him more important?

2. Paul relates divisions in Corinth to moral faults— 'I belong to . . .'. Is such criticism valid for our present situation?

1 Cor 1:17–2:5

No doubt a Corinthian was just as critical of the sermons he had to put up with as we are, and perhaps Paul's preaching had been compared unfavourably with that of Apollos. (*Apolō,* 'I will destroy', begins his quotation from Isaiah in 1 : 19—he could be savage.) Whatever the reason, it provoked this splendid piece of rhetoric against merely human wisdom : 'Jews demand signs and Greeks seek wisdom but we preach Christ crucified' (1 : 22). Neither point is as straightforward as it might seem.

First of all, Jesus certainly is represented by the gospel-writers (John especially) as teaching by signs (*semeia*); that is to say his actions are in the first instance meaningful rather than mere manifestations of power to force men to believe (what, after all, would they then be believing in?). To take one example, the feeding of the multitudes in the desert is : (*a*) part of a sequence designed to show Jesus as the new Moses, for Israel a deeply significant idea (baptism, temptations, feeding, transfiguration take him from the new Red Sea to the new Sinai); (*b*) designed to express the prophetic teaching about the paradise feast in the last day (eg Is 25 : 6–8); and (*c*) expressive of eucharistic teaching. Plenty more examples could be added. Yet at the same time we also have clear rejection of 'signs' in passages such as Lk 11 : 29 : 'this is an evil generation, it seeks a sign'. Presumably what is being rejected there is the power-politics of popular messianic expectation, as in the temptations that open and close the ministry (Lk 4 : 1–13; 23 : 35–39). It is the mistake we make when we present the miracles and the resurrection primarily as 'proofs of divinity'.

With Paul's rejection of human wisdom we come to the other side of the paradox. For Christ is the 'wisdom of God' (1 : 30; cf Jn 1 : 1–18, remembering that *logos*, 'word' (masculine) corresponds to *sophia,* 'wisdom' (feminine)). Once again his human life makes meaningful to us that mystery of God's love which before was hidden but is now made plain (Col 1 : 26—men did their best to cover the mystery up again with elaborate liturgies). We have to work out the meaning of what God has said and done, and since he has used human words and ideas we need not fear to do the same. But this is to seek understanding from within faith, in Augustine's classical phrase. We all do this. No doubt our traditions of interpretation differ, and are what cause our divisions; but we cannot turn our backs on the past, it is there. Perhaps, however, we can ask if some of our traditions have gone too far, others not far enough. The wisdom Paul condemns is that of the Greeks, to whom the resurrection was as big a problem (Acts 17 : 22–34) as the criminal death of Jesus was to the Jews (Gal 3 : 13). To a Greek, with his rational proofs of the immortality of the soul, the body was the last thing one would want back after death. (I hope we are quite sure *we* want it.)

The kind of question Paul's ideas must raise for us today concerns the use of reason in theology. No one would want to prove some part of the faith from reason alone, but some of the arguments in the books look terribly close to it (truth of the gospels→resurrection→ divinity of Christ→infallibility). Then there are those metaphysical 'proofs' that God exists, with the implication that for many they are needed as a prelude to belief. Reason can provide helpful analogies for faith, but perhaps the dangers outweigh the advantages.

1. How much of a contrast is there between baptism and the preaching of Christ?

2. What is the proper balance between faith and rational understanding? Or for that matter between power and weakness?

3. How can christian thinking be made to seem relevant to a world which takes so much account of scientific thought? What is the best approach to the modern unbeliever?

2
Being human
1 Cor 2:6–4:21

1 Cor 2:6–3:3

Paul develops his theme of christian wisdom, maturity in Christ. As he says later, 'Do not be children in your thinking; be babes in evil, but in thinking be mature' (14:20, cf Heb 5:11–14). For him there is no question of the kind of arrested development which passes for spirituality in some later writing, and goes with an exaggerated respect for authority and the desire that somebody else should do all our thinking for us.

This wisdom he is talking about covers moral questions as well as doctrinal ones: Paul does not put them in separate compartments in the way we sometimes do. As we shall see, he gives advice in moral matters, but at the same time he insists that each man's informed conscience makes the final decision (10:23–30). His ideas are perhaps most fully developed in the passage on growing to mature manhood in Christ, 'no longer children tossed to and fro and carried about with every wind of doctrine' (Eph 4:13–16). It is in the light of ideas such as these that we have to understand the gospel statement about 'receiving the kingdom of God like a child' (Mk 10:15). It cannot be the child's immaturity and lack of critical judgement that is being singled out there: more probably it is his receptiveness. But in any case (to illustrate

the greater difficulty of understanding the gospels) it
seems quite likely that Mark has shaped the passage on
account of contemporary divisions of opinion about infant baptism—several technical phrases from the baptismal liturgy appear.

A second point to notice is the insistence once again
that the Spirit has now made clear to us what had previously been secret and hidden (2 : 7). Notice the plurals
throughout this passage. It is the community which is
given new understanding—and at Corinth the community which had failed. We must not imagine from what
Paul is saying here that he envisaged a kind of elite 'in-
group' of the spiritual, with special information withheld
from the ordinary church member. There was already a
strong tendency to this kind of division in those groups,
outside the church, which developed into the gnostics of
the next century; but then, as always, the church bitterly
resisted them. Christian teaching, like christian salvation,
is meant for everyone. The 'fleshly' man (3 : 1) who as
yet has not been able to grasp the full christian message
is someone who has allowed sin to obscure his understanding; the implied division is primarily moral rather
than intellectual. Whatever he may suppose, says Paul,
the man who has not yet, in Christ, managed to overcome
sin is still an immature child in the only wisdom which
matters. We have to get used to this use of terms such as
spiritual and *fleshly* with a moral sense. *Body, soul, spirit,
flesh* in biblical usage are usually not parts of man, but
stand for man in different relations to God. The Spirit
here is sent from God to unite us to Christ so that we
grow into his manhood, grow more human since we 'have
the mind of Christ' (2 : 16).

1. In what way does the Holy Spirit make the faith clear to us?

2. Can we in fact make much of the Spirit as a person distinct from Christ in our thinking?

3. Do we become more human by growing more spiritual?

4. How can we grow in wisdom by growing into Christ?

1 Cor 3:4–23

Paul now finds further metaphors to describe the church. They are metaphors of life and growth. The community is a field which the missionaries plant and water, but God alone makes things grow (3:7); a building founded on Christ, who when he comes will show up the quality of the work (3:13); a living temple to house God in the world and make him present to men (3:16). The contrast between the manufactured and the human temple had already been made by Stephen in Paul's presence (Acts 7): it seems to have been emphasised in the 'hellenist' (? Essene) tradition. John later gave it classical expression at the opening of his gospel (Jn 2:13–22; cf Jn 1:14, with the reference to the 'tent' in the wilderness). Christ and the church united to him are God's presence to the world.

Perhaps this is why Paul then returns once again to the theme of the christian in the world. He first draws the now-familiar contrast between two kinds of wisdom (3:18–20): the christian is a new creation (2 Cor 5:17) and lives a different kind of existence. Yet he is firmly in the world too. It is the johannine balance between 'they are not of the world' yet 'sent into the world' (Jn 17:16–18). Paul is sometimes other-worldly, but always with a certain nuance; deal with the world, he says, as if you had no dealings with it (7:31). Here he splendidly breaks into his 'All things are yours'—everything, world, life, death, present and future, belong to us just because, in Christ, we can stand back from them. We alone can bring the world back to God through Christ, since the world encounters God only by contact with us. 'We are ambassadors for Christ, God making his appeal through us' (2 Cor 5:20). We don't always recognise just how much the world should therefore *matter* to us politically, socially, in our work . . . in the wide sense of the word, *morally*.

    1. What are the points of comparison between the church and the Jewish temple?
    2. Fellow-workers for God? Is it better, other things being equal, to go on working in the world or to preach the gospel?

1 Cor 4:1–21

What is the position of one who has power in the christian community? The new testament gives the answer in clear terms, as Paul does here. A christian leader is never more than a steward under God (4:1—the word is often used by Luke in the parables). God alone possesses all power and authority, but he has given it to Christ in the resurrection (Mt 28:18) now to share with us. But we are only stewards of that power; we can never treat authority as though it were a possession. Even in those days this was easily forgotten: 'if you received it why do you boast as if it were not a gift?' (4:7). Yet with christians the greatest should be the lowest of all (Mt 23:11–12), servant of God's servants. Paul contrasts the situation

of the apostles with those placed under them (4:9–13).
His irony as so often is exaggerated, but even so it forms
a piquant contrast with the situation in some later ages
in the church.

*1. How can we increase the awareness of scripture
within the church, so as truly to live by it?*

*2. Have we paid enough attention in the churches to
the example of Christ's putting-off of what he had by
right?*

3

Christian behaviour
1 Cor 5:1–6:20

1 Cor 5:1–8

We should seriously ask if Paul really took the right line in this matter; certainly our immediate reaction to the situation would be different from his. Was he right to throw the man out of the community? (5:2, cf 5:13). This action will shock us if we think of sin as a private matter between the individual (? soul) and God. Paul doesn't. For him being a christian means living in the one Spirit as a member of God's people, the community of Christ, so that what each person does must directly concern all. The loss of this idea is reflected in the failure of our liturgical life; even where repentance is thought of in sacramental terms it is not expressed in community action. The man's case, notice, is not despaired of; he returns to 'Satan' (the world in the grip of sin) but he may in consequence repent (one supposes) and be saved (5:5).

Again Paul doesn't appeal to any law, not even to the obvious commandment. For him the commandments themselves have been transformed by the new spirit of freedom (2 Cor 3:6—but read the whole chapter). He always returns to the basic truth of what Christ has done and what we have thereby become. 'Christ has been sacrificed' (5:7)—this is why sin should no longer be pos-

sible. The representative man has offered himself to the
Father, and because the offering has been fully accepted,
he and we with him have entered into divine life. It is
like the old leaven of the Jewish passover (5 : 7–8)—there
is no place for that when the new leaven has come in. We
have become something quite new, and so it follows that
we will behave in a new way (a consequence rather than
an obligation). Behaviour is always the test of what one
is; if men sin gravely no change in them ever took place.
Recognise this and leave the church, he says!

*1. What about this decision to cut the man off from the
community? Is there any justification for such action
today?*

*2. How can we relate Paul's attitude to morality with
the rigid moral codes of modern christianity?*

*3. Do we find it difficult to think about sin in com-
munity terms, and if so should we be doing anything
about it?*

1 Cor 5:9–6:11

This might seem rather an arbitrary division—is there
much connection between the different ideas in it? I
think so. Paul first talks about the christian community
in relation to the world at large. For reasons we have just
seen, the church must purge itself so far as possible of
sinful elements (5 : 11), but not avoid all contact with the
sinful world (5 : 9). The community of Christ isn't 'out of
this world,' but in living communion with it, 'that the
world may believe' (Jn 17 : 21).

There is a natural connection, then, with the next
part, the use of secular law-courts (6 : 1–8). We do not face

the same problem, of course, but we do have the difficulty
that secular law may well conflict with christian moral
belief. More particularly, when the churches themselves
do not agree about moral decisions we should avoid the
simple identification of the areas of sin and crime, bringing pressure to bear on the legislature to extend the latter
area to the former; their relationship is subtle and demands discussion.

As usual Paul places the matter in the context of much
more general theological ideas. He thinks at once of the
final judgement of God. His perspective differs signifi-
cantly from that of the average christian today in two
respects. First, because for him judgement concerns the
community, and the individual is judged according as he
is a member of it or not. God's judgement separates off
those who are in Christ from those who aren't. (This of
course raises considerable problems about who, in fact, is
a member of the church, and how; problems which we
all have to face at some time or other.) John develops this
point of view to its full extent; men enter the judgement
of salvation or of condemnation according as they recognise or refuse 'the light' which is Christ, and believe or
not. 'This is the judgement, that the light has come into
the world, and men loved darkness rather than light, because their deeds were evil' (Jn 3 : 19; cf Jn 8 : 12–16).
No doubt it is this connection between judgement and
community which here leads Paul to associate the church
with the fact of judgement in a way that may strike us as
odd (6 : 2–3).

Even odder perhaps—and this is the second difference
—is the way the new testament tends to look at the present in terms of the future. Essentially *judgement* means
the collective one on the coming 'day of our Lord Jesus

Christ' (1:7; cf 2 Cor 5:10). Yet there are more 'particular' occasions of judgement, because the force of this one judgement has already broken into our world through the death and resurrection of Christ. Hence the gospels present the cross itself as a final judgement scene; cf the imagery of Lk 23:44 or Mt 27:51–53 with that of passages such as Joel 2: 30–31, quoted at Pentecost. And signs of the judgement are also associated with 'secular' events such as the destruction of Jerusalem, cf Lk 21:20–28. We should realise that any serious (ie moral) decision on our part introduces us into the sphere of the future judgement because it alters our relationship to the community of Christ. That is why for John judgement is both now and hereafter (eg Jn 12:31 and 12:48).

A point worth noting (because a false tradition to the contrary is still common) is that christians, far from being forbidden to judge one another, are required by Paul to do so for their mutual benefit. Against this one is usually referred to the gospel saying 'judge not that you be not judged' (sc 'by God'). (The lips are tightly drawn together in disapproval!) That the saying hangs loose in the gospels (Mt 7:1–2 puts it in a somewhat different context from Lk 6:37) should put us on our guard about interpreting it over-simply, as should the lukan gloss which substitutes 'condemn' for 'judge', and the parable which in each gospel follows at once: the point of getting the log out of our own eye seems to be that we should see clearly enough to get the splinter out of our brother's, ie judge him impartially.

Paul's last point here touches on the question of justification (6:11) worked out more fully in Romans. Here too the community perspective we have been taking helps us to understand his meaning. It was Israel, the people,

who of old were justified by God through the great acts
of salvation accomplished in them. Now the final action of
God in Christ has brought into existence a new justified
community, the church. It is this justified community
that each of us enters by faith in Christ, normally required and given in baptism ('you were washed', 6 : 11),
together with holiness ('you were sanctified'), because the
community is holy (of course both faith and holiness
must manifest themselves in our life). Justification is by
faith for Paul because this is how we personally enter
the objective saving situation made for us by God in
Christ: 'and this is not your own doing, it is the gift of
God—not because of works, lest any man should boast'
(Eph 2 : 8).

1. *What is the real line in the new testament on judg-
ing one another?*

2. *The judgement is to come. Then how are we justified now?*

3. *Who has the right to judge? If the church is to judge
with Christ, doesn't this call for a new realisation of
community with him?*

4. *What sort of attitude are we to take to the law of the
state? Is it right for christians to try to change it?*

1 Cor 6 : 12–20

We need not spend too long on this section, which contains ideas which have been or will be developed more
fully elsewhere. It is hard for people to be free, or even
to want freedom. Then, as now, the great pauline teaching on freedom in Christ was misunderstood, and while
the Galatians wanted to get back under the shelter of the

law, the Corinthians saw an excuse for lawlessness (6:12). Paul seems to have fornication particularly in mind as their chief temptation (RSV 'immorality' is hardly a satisfactory translation, unless it is now Standard American) and this may be why his mind moves to two of his central themes; relationship to Christ as a member of his body and as bride. Only when we are united in this way with Christ through his community do we share in the act of salvation by which God 'raised the Lord' (6:14). The phrase 'become one spirit' with Christ (6:17) would not have seemed out of place for Paul in such a context of *bodily* union. We are united bodily to Christ in the Spirit whom he sends to share his life with us, who dwells in us as in a temple (6:19).

1. 'Glorify God in your body.' What does this say about Paul's views on morality?

2. Can one reconcile the modern notion of natural law with 'all things are lawful'?

4

The law of Christ
1 Cor 7:1–9:23

1 Cor 7:1–40

The first sentence is important. Paul is answering particular questions he'd been asked. He is not producing a
text-book on the theology of marriage. What he says here
needs to be balanced by the later passage on marriage as
an entry into, and expression of, Christ's relationship
with his church (Eph 5:21–33). It will help us to understand this rather miscellaneous collection of statements if
we see in the background the central idea of the christian
community as Christ's bride.

Next we ought to notice the eschatological flavour to
Paul's thought. 'The appointed time has grown very
short' (7:29); 'the form of this world is passing away'
(7:31). It says more than that this world hasn't much
longer to go, though this is certainly part of Paul's
thought. Things have to be looked at in the light of the
age which is coming, whose effect is already at work in
the present age. Now in the age to come our relationship
with Christ will be more direct; we shall see 'face to face'
(13:12). Marriage itself will not be needed then (cf Mt
22:30): its importance is that it reflects the future relationship of union with Christ, but direct union is better
still. Can we then perhaps see the choice (or even just the

acceptance) of virginity in this world as an attempt to achieve that future relationship on earth, at least to a greater extent than marriage makes possible? Certainly Paul here sees virginity as a christian ideal (eg 7:7, 26, 32, 38), and this aspect of his thought has been taken up in catholic teaching about the 'greater perfection of a state of virginity'. It should be remembered that Paul's views do not actually attack marriage, nor deny that particular married people may not be closer to God than particular celibates are—'let everyone lead the life which the Lord has assigned to him, and in which God has called him', he says wisely (7:17). But we can still be glad about Ephesians, even if it was one of Paul's pupils who wrote it.

We need not spend too much time on Paul's decisions about the matters that had been put to him; the last thing he would have wanted us to do would be to take them as final decisions for all time. But we might notice the phrase, which he uses elsewhere too, 'not I, but the Lord' (7:10). This refers, not to a direct message from Christ, but to the tradition of the church, which he was not free to change. In this passage the tradition unequivocally rejects divorce. The contrast then follows, 'I say, not the Lord'. Here Paul speaks in his own right, as an apostle (7:12). And here we find an anticipation of the teaching in Ephesians. Marriage is such that even when it is 'mixed' christian-pagan the two partners are consecrated by being one flesh (7:14), and the association may well be the means of salvation for the pagan (7:16). We can remember this when joining issue with him over passages such as 7:34, and in any case a lot can be forgiven a man capable of producing the splendid understatement with which the section ends (7:40).

1. Is it possible to tie up Paul's various views on marriage, or are we to say he changed his mind?

2. Is the implication of 7 : 14 that all marriage between christians is sacramental? Certainly some churches don't seem to accept this. On what grounds?

1 Cor 8:1–13

The issue discussed here and taken up again in Chapter 10 was clearly a very important one for the first communities; the apostles laid it down as one of the few 'necessary things' that christians should 'abstain from what has been sacrificed to idols' (Acts 15 : 29); in practice this would mean most of the meat on sale in a city. The Jews had their own butchers' shops, which the christians could have used, or alternatively set up their own ('catholic mutton from catholic sheep'): the question they wanted Paul to answer was whether such action was necessary. As they realised that idols did not exist, they could eat the meat in question without scruple.

The argument was one that would appeal to Paul, convinced as he was that in Christ we are freed from all scrupulous legal observance, and in principle he therefore agrees with the questioners, typically setting out basic trinitarian ideas in order to do so (8 : 4–6). But at the same time his sympathetic mind recognises how easily these 'enlightened' christians could harm their brothers who had not yet been able to overcome superstition. A responsible man's conscience doesn't work in a vacuum, but within the community, and the community must always be taken into account. We may have to renounce acting in accordance with our superior knowledge in order to build up the community in love (8 : 1, 9–13).

We have to judge things in the light of what will be done to 'the brother for whom Christ died' (8:11). The line Paul takes obviously applies to a lot of situations nearer home. But he doesn't suggest that we should suppress the truth, because it might cause scandal; only that we should refrain from an action, harmless in itself, if it will cause scandal. The two are not always very clearly separated in people's minds.

1. Ought we to distinguish between knowing and loving God?

2. How does a christian serve God in the world?

3. Do we put our emphasis on avoiding scandal in the right place?

1 Cor 9:1–23

The thought that christians do not have to claim the privileges their freedom gives them seems to have set Paul off on this rather long digression concerning what he could have claimed as an apostle if he'd wanted to (9:1–18). Notice the two-fold claim for apostleship: Paul had made direct physical contact with the risen Lord (cf 1 Jn 1:1–2), and the guarantee of its genuineness was the Corinthian church that he had founded (9:1–2). Now an apostle has the right to claim the support of the church for himself and his wife (Paul's is a typically rabbinic interpretation of Deut 25:4). But he waives any such rights. In fact he could not do other than preach the gospel, irrespective of reward (9:16–17). And his real reward is that the gospel is freely given to all (9:18).

So his thought, as so often, turns to the question of christian freedom (9:19–23). By entering into our human situation, Christ converted it from the state of bondage to sin and alienation from God into a state of obedience and love. So, in paradoxical language, 'You who were once slaves of sin . . . have become slaves of righteousness' (Rom 6:17). This new situation of reconciliation to God means redemption from the bonds which chained us: 'For freedom Christ has set us free' (Gal 5:1). This freedom means release from the burden of the law which, though it was good, must be included among the powers that enslaved us (such as sin and death) because it was powerless to free men from the sinfulness which at the same time it made clear to them (Rom 7:7—NB the context of all these passages really needs to be read as well). Only when we have rejected all reliance on our power to keep the law shall we be relying on Christ alone. We have to let go, recognise that of ourselves we cannot deal with our sinfulness, and then we shall have gained Christ fully. 'For his sake I have suffered the loss of all things, and count them as refuse, in order that I may gain Christ and be found in him, not having a righteousness of my own, based on law, but that which is through faith in Christ' (Phil 3:8–9).

Then what does Paul mean by what he here calls 'the law of Christ' (9:21) or elsewhere 'the law of the Spirit' (Rom 8:2)? Certainly not a new set of obligations, not even the 'new commandments' which summarise the old law (Mt 22:37–40). Not something which can be set out in statement at all, but rather a new life in Christ brought by the Spirit. Certainly it is a life of serving God through one's neighbour, but no longer because of some obligation to do so. The reference is plain enough in the words Paul was later to send to Corinth: 'You are a letter from Christ delivered by us, written not with ink but with the Spirit of the living God, not on tablets of stone but on tablets of human hearts' (2 Cor 3:3). Freedom from law means not lawlessness but new responsibility, new maturity.

1. Do we really agree with Paul's notion of christian freedom? Or is it too ideal for man?

2. Paul seems to agree with the compiler of the 'sermon on the mount' that the old commands are done with. But would he have wanted to replace them by a new set? And what would he have said about the church's selective disregard for these (oaths are back in, not divorce)?

5

The worship of the church
1 Cor 9:24–11:34

1 Cor 9:24–10:13

Paul is still considering the question of idolatry; but for him moral questions must be viewed in a sacramental context. He begins with a straightforward warning against assuming that it is no longer possible for christians to fall into sin (9:24–27), and deals with it in terms of the prototype situation in which Israel at the time of the exodus could commit sin despite their covenant relationship with God, expressed here in the sacramental terms of christian baptism and eucharist.

This raises some difficulty for us. We can now, as a result of the work of the scholars, analyse the scriptural accounts of an event such as the exodus, and see how Israel's understanding of the event developed through its history, so that the various strands of thought in the pentateuch differ among themselves, and differ from the tradition recorded in other parts of the bible, eg in a historical psalm like Ps 105. When these accounts are set against the historical situations in which they grew up, a great deal of light is shed on their meaning. But the rabbinical tradition to which Paul belonged was in no position to do this; instead, it attempted to smooth out the differences and synthesise them into a factual account of what was thought to have occurred, in a way that will be familiar at any rate to catholics from old-fashioned commentators such as Knox. We have to accept that typical new testament interpretations of the old testament may need considerable modification in the light of present knowledge.

In 10 : 1, the cloud relates back to passages like Ex 13 : 21 (the 'under' probably shows the influence of Ps 105 : 39). It had become the traditional sign of God's presence : we can recall the clouds of Christ's baptism, transfiguration, ascension. The (Red) sea is a second reminder of God's saving hand (Ex 14 : 21). Paul naturally thinks of the similarities to christian baptism (cf his remarks at Rom 6 : 3), for the new community in Christ is brought into a covenant relationship with God just as the old Israel had been through Moses. In the same way he relates (10 : 3) the miraculous feeding of the people by Moses in the wilderness (Ex 16) to the eucharist, rather as the gospel accounts of Christ's miraculous feeding (eg in Jn 6) relate it back to Moses and forward to the eucharist. Paul also adds an exodus parallel to the eucharistic drink : the water which flowed from the rock when it was struck by Moses (Ex 17 : 1–7). This story already existed in such a mixed-up complex of traditions in the old testament, several different locations for the event being given, that the rabbis had ingeniously suggested that the rock followed Israel around in the way the pillar of cloud did : Paul accepts their tradition here. Moreover, the rock could be identified with God himself : in Ex 17 : 6 it seems to be thought of as a throne on which God stood, rather as the ark was in the earliest tradition, and it is interesting to notice how naturally Paul extends the identification in 10 : 4 from God to Christ, presumably thought of as existing from the beginning (cf Col 1 : 15–17).

This passage has been considered in some detail as an illustration of the complexity, yet the value, involved in working out fully a fairly typical piece of new-testament theological thinking. Paul, however, simply uses it as a warning (10:5–10) of what can happen to us, on whom the triumphant victory of Christ which marks the end of history has already broken in (10:11) making us closer in him to God than even Israel was.

1. How have christians managed to make any sense of the new testament without reading much of the old testament if the connection is so close?

2. Paul asks for a fuller realisation of what the liturgy means. How does this relate to present practice?

3. Does the church's worship today help us to reach a community that does not take notice of divisions of class or race? Does it look beyond itself to the world?

1 Cor 10:14–11:1

The meat question can now be treated at a deeper level. As he has already said, the idols themselves are nothing (10:19), and so we can eat whatever we fancy without being scrupulous (10:25–27). Yet behind the idols, in fact behind the whole pagan state, there is the reality of the evil spirits in whom Paul firmly believed (10:20), as did our Lord himself (eg in Mk 3:22–27). Now to offer sacrifice to devils is to enter into relationship with them. Hence when a christian is worried about the situation, and specifically voices the question of eating sacrificial meat, his scruple is not purely imaginary, and it is better to renounce one's freedom for his sake (10:24, 28–29).

The reference to the eucharist (10:16–18, 21) comes almost casually into the middle of the argument. No christian could share a sacrificial meal with pagans because he shares the meal of the sacrificed Lord. The idea behind sacrifice in Israel was that it united the worshipper with God, to whom it was offered, provided that God accepted it (and hence the moral demand of a right heart; acceptance was not automatic). Acceptance meant that the offering, and so too the offerer, was now charged with the divine power, the presence of God to them, above all if the offering was later eaten. In 10:18, 'partners in the altar' means 'partners with God' who was often referred to by such circumlocutions. Now it is clear that the christian eucharist is not directly a sacrifice in this sense: for us there is only one sacrifice, which can never be repeated (cf Rom 6:9). For all that, the eucharist was thought of in sacrificial terms, as the present context, and the language of blood and of body, show. The cup and the bread give us a share (*koinonia* = fellowship, communion) in the body and blood of the sacrificed and risen Lord (10:16–17). *Body* here has several related senses. The body which is the church is constituted by its members sharing in the body which is the bread they break (10:17). Behind both these senses is *body* meaning the physical body (person) of the risen Christ. As men share in the meal his presence to them links them to him and to one another: here all three ways of speaking—eucharistic body, physical body, and church body—are closely united.

Perhaps this is the point to discuss the problem that later developments have raised; granted that the church is Christ's body in a real sense, though not the physical body which is his personally before the Father, is this true of the eucharistic body as well, or is the word there used only metaphorically? Popular catholic thinking is often grossly over-physical at this point. In the case of the church, to say that it is really Christ is still to leave room for a distinction which is marked by the use of words like *mystical* or *sacramental* (*sacramentum* is the Latin equivalent of the Greek *mystērion,* and in modern theology the church is often spoken of as a sacrament, rather as Christ is himself the sacrament of God). Christ's presence to his church is not the presence of his natural, physical being as we shall see it in heaven, yet it is completely real. We can properly think of it as a kind of extension of his bodily presence into our world, brought about through the thoroughly material and bodily words and gestures of the liturgy. We may then be inclined to agree that Paul is also thinking realistically of the eucharistic body, and genuinely identifying it with Christ, yet in such a way that *real* does not mean 'natural and physical, though in no way visible'. The same distinction as that between the natural body and the church body will still have to be made; indeed up to the twelfth century the word *mystical* was used for this purpose, though now *sacramental* seems more normal when speaking of the eucharistic body.

1. *The reformers totally rejected the idea of sacrifice in the eucharist, but against them the Council of Trent strongly reaffirmed it. How could they both have been right?*

2. *In modern English usage* mystical *means something very different from* sacramental. *How far has the modern sense of* mystical *been misused in the interpretation of ideas like 'the mystical body of Christ'?*

1 Cor 11:2–16

The less said about this passage the better, though it won't be. The reason for it is probably that christian men had felt they were free not to follow the Jewish custom of covering the head when praying, and women had rashly done the same. Unfortunately, unveiled women were usually no better than they ought to be, especially in Corinth, and Paul's ruling is just common sense for the time. But here his habit of giving theological reasons for practical counsel at last catches up with him, and he is betrayed into some peculiar arguments for the inferiority of women, which only 11 : 11–12 helps to mitigate.

Need we pay any attention to an apostle's views on these matters, or can they just be dismissed as irrelevant?

1 Cor 11:17–34

He now moves on to talk more directly of the eucharist. In Corinth, at least, it was combined with a social meal or *agapē,* which it seems to have followed. By the time the gospels were being written this had probably disappeared, perhaps because of abuses mentioned here. Instead of sharing their provisions with the whole community, the richer members seem to have finished them off before the others arrived (11 : 21), no doubt after a day's work. How can men who are behaving unjustly in this way eat the Lord's supper together? (11 : 17–22). Today we do not make our social divisions so obvious at the eucharist, or not at any rate in Europe, but certainly there is still very little positive manifestation of the unity between the celebrants which it is the ultimate purpose of the action to bring about. The catholic mass, for instance, has ceased to be a performance watched passively by a crowd of individuals, and become nearer to what it should be, an action in which everyone present has a full part to play: we may still wonder how effectively this will constitute us a living body in any higher sense than that in which other mutual aid societies work. 'Each one goes ahead with his own meal' (11:21).

So Paul repeats the church's tradition ('I received from the Lord,' 11:23) of the institution of the supper. It is the earliest account: Luke's seems to be fairly close to it (Lk 22:19–20), but Mark (Mk 14:22–24) and, following him, Matthew (Mt 26:26–27) differ appreciably. This, as we have seen, is typical of scripture: we cannot hope to reconstruct the event to which the accounts point back, though the similarities behind the differences in fact make its historicity more certain than if we had but a single tradition. Though the authors are describing the last supper, what they have in mind is the contemporary liturgy; though occasional details of the supper have been kept—Paul and Luke, for instance, tell us that the cup was blessed 'after supper' though in Mark this has dropped out—for the most part the repeatable, formal elements are alone described.

In both traditions these essential elements are the taking of bread, thanksgiving, breaking, and distribution; similarly for the wine. Thanksgiving, in Israel's tradition, is equivalent to blessing: when we acknowledge, by giving thanks to God, that something belongs to him, he takes it and makes it his, that is, he makes it holy and blessed (it is the idea behind sacrifice, as we have seen). The blessed bread and wine are shared by the community so that they too enter the divine holiness: cf the earliest account of the covenant in Ex 24:11, in which the people eat and drink in the presence of God. But the blessedness is now the presence of God's Son. What has made this meal of union an effective reality is the new covenant relationship established in Christ with God by the resurrection, directly referred to in the words said over the cup—'this is the new covenant in my blood'. The reference is to a second account of the sealing of the original covenant, Ex 24:3–8, in which blood was sprinkled first on the altar (representing God) and then on the people, as symbol of the union between them. The blood of Christ has now made that union permanent. In Paul the phrase had not yet come into line with the words said over the bread: 'This is the new covenant', rather than 'This is my blood', indicates more clearly how the relationship is being made effectively present. The old testament itself had looked forward to this: eg Jer 31:31–4 speaks of a law written no longer on stones but in men's hearts.

'Do this in remembrance of me' is probably a further covenant reference: the passover feast had been a memorial of the exodus events (Ex 13:9). The Hebrew word for *remembrance* which lies behind this meant more than mere reminder. The action being remembered is made present in an effective way (cf the usage in 1 Kgs 17:18). Notice too the eschatological significance of Paul's comment, 'You proclaim the Lord's death until he comes'. It is Christ risen, filled with the Father's glory, who is present to the church as they eat and drink with him, so that the meal is a reminder and pledge of that direct encounter which we shall have after his return (cf Mk 14:25 for the same idea expressed in other terms). The early church was more aware than we of the way in which our future is anticipated in the eucharistic action.

Finally we must keep in mind the connection already established by Paul (10:17) between the eucharistic body and the church body. We eat the one in order to become more fully the other. Probably both are included in the warning which follows about eating and drinking 'without discerning the body' (11:29). Sinners fail to recognise the relationship of love which binds men into a body with Christ; it is no use their trying to enter it by share in the eucharist if their continuing sin contradicts the meaning of their action. Paul connects the situation with the presence of sickness and death in the community; though a relationship between sin and death is established in Gen 3:16–19 (cf Rom 5:2), the directness of the connection here is a bit startling.

1. How do we best 'proclaim the Lord's death until he comes'? What importance has his final coming for our present lives?

2. Can we take seriously the connection between wrong-doing and physical illness? Isn't it the good who die young?

3. Why do you suppose that the eucharist had been separated from a meal in this gentile church (only recently, so that traces remain which the later gospel accounts have lost)? Remember the character of meals in Jewish thought.

6

The life of the Spirit
1 Cor 12:1–14:20

1 Cor 12:1–13:12

At first sight this whole section must seem pretty remote; 'speaking with tongues' has ceased to be the problem it was in Corinth. Perhaps what is oddest about these early days of enthusiasm is the way in which powers that seem remarkable to us and others that seem quite ordinary are mixed together on the same level; wisdom and miracles, knowledge and speaking with tongues (12:8–10). In this section Paul insists that behind them all lies the power of the one Holy Spirit, sent by God through the risen Lord (12:4–6). It is natural to Paul to think in this trinitarian way, and equally to introduce the idea by the liturgical formula 'Jesus is Lord' (12:3), the great declaration of faith in the resurrection made from the earliest times (cf Acts 2:36), since the raising up of Jesus by the Father raised up the community into the Father's presence through the sending of the Spirit (Rom 8:11). Spiritual gifts could easily divide up the community, if those who enjoyed the more spectacular ones thought themselves better than the rest (we still suffer from sodalities, guilds, and other élite bodies in the church). Paul therefore develops his plea for unity in the Spirit into an image of the community as a body with different members, all of which are needed if the whole is to work properly (12:12–27). Community always comes before individual.

The metaphor of the 'body politic' was a commonplace in the ancient world, but here it is given a deeper meaning. If 12:12 had ended in the way we'd expect ('so it is with the church') this would still be metaphor; in fact Paul says 'so it is with Christ'. There is a real identity between Christ risen and the church, because of the Spirit sent to unite them. Later on Paul was to work out more carefully the theology of the relationship in terms of head and members (eg Col 1:18, 24, etc). Here he is more concerned with the practical point that 'the members may have the same care one for another' (12:25). God's gifts are less for us personally than for the community as a whole—a truth each age has to learn afresh.

So Paul returns to his list of church officers, putting them in order of importance; today we might translate into 'bishops, theologians, catechists, miracle workers (abroad), faith-healers (anointing the sick is still taken seriously), the clericalised laity, and the over-spiritual or fey'. Perhaps by reaction from these, he breaks into the famous hymn on love (13:1–13). Love is the greatest of the Spirit's gifts. That it is a gift at all might surprise us: aren't all men capable of it? Not the love which Paul is talking about, love which 'does not insist on its own way' (13:5), love which is always giving to others. But he doesn't mean a pale and fleshless spiritual love; he would certainly have included the physical love between man and wife. The love of which he speaks is fully human, because it comes (even to those who do not recognise its source) from the human risen Christ, who came into the world to give us back this power to love. He died in order that being raised up he could give his love to all in the

Spirit, so that all, through their love of others, could offer it back to the Father, having been made sons. 'In this is love, not that we loved God but that he loved us and sent his son . . .' (1 Jn 4:10). John's epistle is the best commentary on 1 Cor 13.

1. How can these rather out of the way accomplishments be of any interest to the ordinary christian?

2. Is there in fact a value in divisions, either in a particular church or among christians generally?

3. Can we love to order?

1 Cor 14:1–37

We needn't worry about the details of this passage, after what has gone before. Paul is insisting on the primacy of prophecy over 'speaking with tongues'. By 'prophecy' he seems to mean teaching the things of faith intelligibly; the new-testament prophets were not crystal-gazers, any more than the old-testament ones. 'Speaking with tongues' probably covers many sorts of ecstatic and unintelligible utterance. What we need to realise is that Paul is talking throughout about the liturgy (14:26). Certainly 14:26–33 gives a vivid impression of active and spontaneous participation by every member of the congregation. There is no sign of the false idea that spiritual gifts are the prerogative of those in charge. We no longer need, for the most part, Paul's warning to run things 'decently and in order' (14:40); spontaneity in modern churches, except for a few off-beat ones, is either absent or carefully prepared. But the chapter also shows us the threat to the liturgy presented by two abuses still common enough: mystification and private devotion. Paul's preference for prophecy over tongues is directed against both of these. The new testament prophet or teacher spoke to the whole assembly for their benefit in their own language; the speaker of tongues merely directed attention to himself even when he could be interpreted. Just as today, dislike for community and dislike for the mind went together; romantic appeals to the peasants' simple faith on the part of the sophisticated are usually associated with refusals to participate 'in case it might destroy the mystery'. For Paul these attitudes are signs of immaturity. 'Do not be children in your thinking: be babes in evil, but in thinking be mature' (14:20). 'He who speaks in a tongue edifies himself, but he who prophesies edifies the church' (14:4).

1. Why this stress on prophecy? What is really meant, especially in relation to the old testament prophets?

2. Is all this a good argument for vernacular liturgies?

3. Is the present structure of our worship too rigid? Should there be more room for spontaneity?

7

The risen man
1 Cor 15:1–16:24

1 Cor 15:1–34

This section begins with a reminder, introduced in fairly solemn terms (15:1–2) of the basic christian beliefs, set out as a kind of creed (15:3–7). As it must be pre-pauline, and probably goes back to the very earliest christian community of the years just after the resurrection, it is of great interest to us. It can usefully be compared with the rather more elaborate forms set out as sermons in Acts (Acts 2:14–39; 3:12–26; 4:9–12; 5:29–32; 10:34–43; 13:16–41)—it was out of such skeleton outlines that the first gospel must have been built up. Of course the pre-occupations are not those of the church which constructed the creeds three centuries later. Christ died for our sins 'according to the scriptures'—almost certainly the redemptive suffering of the servant of God in Is 53 is being thought of. He was buried—an odd emphasis to us, which may well come from thinking of the baptismal liturgy with its burial symbolism, cf Rom 6:4. He was raised on the third day 'according to the scriptures'. In the early church and for Paul it is the Father who raises up Christ: for later theologians he raises himself up (eg Jn 10:18). The old testament support for 'the third day' is probably (though not very happily, to our minds) Hos 6:2. Next comes the apostolic witness to the truth of the

45

event (15:5–8). Though, as we shall see, it was important
to have reliable evidence of this, the theological implications go much deeper. Those who had enjoyed direct contact with Christ risen stood in a privileged position in
relation to the church for all time. This is why Paul,
here (15:8–10) and elsewhere, insists that he belongs to
their number. For they receive the faith of the church
directly from Christ (Gal 1:11–12). Later, at the end of
the apostolic age, the fourth gospel insists even more
clearly on the distinction between those who believe because they have seen and those who believe because of
the words of others who have seen (Jn 17:20; Jn 20:29;
cf 1 Jn 1:1–2). It is this distinction that later still led
the church to determine a canon of new testament scripture on the basis of apostolicity. All later interpretation
had to be referred to this, for by contrast with revelation
it is only the tradition of men, even though we may believe that it is reached with the assistance of the Holy
Spirit.

All this is preliminary to the point Paul wishes to
make: the central importance of the resurrection. If
Christ has not been raised, then all faith is without meaning (15:14). Why are witnesses so important? There is
no trace in the new testament of the later apologetic line
of argument which made the resurrection a 'proof' of
divinity, and based all else on the flat, uncriticised statements of our Lord in the gospels, eliminating automatically the deep and subtle theological insights that we've
begun to recover only in our own times. Yet while the
meaning of the resurrection was not arbitrarily restricted
by the early church to the bare fact that it happened and
so somehow proved that Christ (but not Lazarus, etc) was
God, that it did happen was still essential. The resur-

rection was never interpreted symbolically, its factualness demythologised away. A statement which nothing could ever prove false is simply vacuous, so modern English philosophers would argue; perhaps it is well that an insistence that this event *happened* is thoroughly rooted in the early christian tradition.

Paul's particular concern is to reassure the Corinthians about their own future life. Of his converts the Pharisaic Jews may have taken the resurrection too materialistically, but without question the Greeks, like ourselves, would have been inclined to spiritualise it away. People who identify themselves with their soul are only too willing to have the body drop off; it is easier for most of us to recite the opening statements of the creed with conviction than the closing ones. The Hebrew tradition allowed no such division in man and whatever difficulties this made for personal survival were overcome (until after the Babylonian exile) by the strong sense of community in which a man's descendants guaranteed that he would in some sense live on. The gospels have made us familiar with the Sadducean denial of a resurrection; a view probably that of the majority in bible times. It is perfectly possible to live to God in this world without any hope of future life, and we need to realise this in order to combat the prevalent false christian theology concerned with nothing but future pie. Paul strikes a balance. The least acquaintance with the new testament should be enough to make clear the over-riding importance of this life; yet 'if for this life only we have hoped in Christ, we are of all men most to be pitied' (15:19).

In fact Christ's resurrection, body and soul, is the guarantee of ours. Paul uses the favourite image of first fruits (15:20; cf Col 1:18), the Genesis word for *begin-*

ning. The man Christ begins a new creation, reversing
what the first Adam had done (15 : 21–22; cf Rom 5).
(How impoverished by comparison is the modern popular theologising in which all this is simply related to the
work of Christ as God.) The resurrection begins the
break-in of the end-time, when Christ will return; between the beginning and the end the church's situation is ambiguous. Christ rules over it; but it is still in
the midst of the world. Now the world is by no means
simply alien; Christ is its Lord also (Col 15–17). But he
rules the world through the intermediary creation of the
spiritual powers which we simply must take seriously if
we are to make any sense whatever of the new testament.
These powers, on the whole evil, have ruled the world
since Adam's fall gave them the sovereignty which should
have been human, not spiritual: but the resurrection has,
in Paul's view, put them in a more ambivalent situation,
an exact reflection of the way in which the non-christian
world is to be viewed. On the whole they have been reduced to accepting the power of Christ (the clearest statement of this is in Heb 1 : 14, which Paul would surely
have agreed with), yet they are always liable to break free
and show their old evil character, until the end comes.
Thus the sting of death has been drawn (15 : 55–57)
though it, like sin and law, which Paul includes by a kind
of personification among these ambiguous powers, is still
active in men. Don't let's be afraid of the world and the
world's values (he is saying in effect)—certainly don't let's
withdraw from them; yet remember too that they can go
sour on us, can demand that pinch of incense to the god-
head of Caesar. This probably explains the rather difficult distinction in 15 : 24 between the kingdom of Christ,
in which the angelic creation (rule, authority, power) still

subsists, and the future kingdom of God, when he is quite directly to be 'everything to everyone' (15:28). Even with the background sketched out above, these few verses are far from easy to make much of, and we should be especially careful to avoid slick distinctions of a later age, fearful that Paul might not be orthodox on the Trinity.

No one seems to have the faintest idea what 15:29 really means, though the use Paul makes of it is clear enough. The mormon interpretation, which is of course the literal one, may well be right, though a more attractive idea refers it to those who were baptised on account of the martyrs whose example had drawn them into the church and whom they wanted to rejoin in heaven. The only snag is that there are unlikely to have been martyrs in Corinth as yet. Fortunately, Paul doesn't recommend whatever he refers to, and passes on to some straightforward moral persuasion to accepting resurrection in Christ (15:30–34).

1. What is the real importance of these post-resurrection appearances of Christ?

2. If the crucifixion expiated our sins, what does Paul mean by saying our faith is futile unless Christ has been raised?

3. What is meant by the statement that Christ's resurrection begins the kingdom on earth for us?

1 Cor 15:35–58

Paul refuses to be drawn on the question of what it will be like after death, an unanswerable question on which foolish people have wasted their time ever since (15:35). All that can be said is that there will be recognisable continuity, as between seed and plant; we shall still, then, be embodied, though not in our earthly flesh with all its limitations (15:37). Another way of putting it is that the body will then be *spiritual* rather than *physical* (15:44). *Physical* translates the Greek word for the life-principle of living things on earth; *natural,* or *earthly,* is all that is meant. *Spiritual* is certainly not the same as *disembodied* : it relates to the Holy Spirit whom we already partly possess on earth, and says not much more than *heavenly* : Paul is giving very little away.

The next verses (15:45–49) aren't easy. The contrast is between the 'natural' man Adam, made of the dust (Gen 2:7) though in God's image (Gen 1:27), and the 'heavenly' man Christ, source of the Holy Spirit, who makes us also men of heaven. Quite likely he is attacking a false rabbinic exegesis which divided the two Genesis references between two distinct Adams, an earthly and a heavenly one, of which the heavenly came first. No one, it must be remembered, knew at the time that the contrast in fact represents different traditions written down some four centuries apart. Paul rightly insists that there was only one Adam, an earthly one, in Genesis, and that the Adam of heaven came second, coming not at the beginning of human history, but at its mid-point. The general thought is clear enough: we shall bear the new image, share the glory of the risen Lord (15:49).

So much for the dead: what of the living when Christ returns (15:52)? This was a pretty immediate question for men at the time, still hourly expecting his coming. Perhaps in nuclear times we may instead legitimately doubt whether anyone will actually be alive when he comes. If there are any, they will share in the new life too, just as will the dead, says Paul (15:52), and ends on a fine rhetorical note.

1. Does it make any marked difference to us here and now that we shall live with Christ not as disembodied souls but as human beings?

2. What is the relation between sin, death, and resurrection?

1 Cor 16:1–24

As usual, he returns at once to a practical point—the collection for the poor in the Jerusalem church (16:1–2), frequently mentioned in his letters. He has been writing about unity in a single church, but it must be extended to all. There's no other way to love God than unity and love with our brothers in Christ. So it is no accident that after various personal messages the letter ends with a strong echo of the liturgy (16:20–24). It has been suggested that at the back of Paul's mind was a definite piece of dialogue which had already been formalised, and which has been reconstructed as follows from later accounts:

V. Let grace come and the world pass away.
R. Hosanna to the God of David.
If any man is holy let him come
If any man is not let him depart
V. Come, Lord.
R. Amen.

Liturgy and doctrine, doctrine and life: for the early church these were no catch phrases, but aspects of a single way of life intensely lived. Our reading of 1 Corinthians

should have set us asking how we can recover something
of this for our own day.

    *1. How will liturgical reform and development help us
to re-establish the connection between liturgy and life?*

    *2. Why does it matter that we should re-establish the
connection?*

2 Corinthians

Henry Wansbrough

Introduction

By way of prologue to introduce the reader to the situation, it is necessary to say a word about Corinth and a word about Paul. Corinth was a port town on the isthmus joining the southern peninsula of Greece to the mainland. Through this town and across the narrow isthmus passed a very large volume of trade going chiefly from the eastern part of the empire to the capital at Rome. Hence Corinth was richly supplied with all the seamier side of life associated with dockland. As trade flourished, there was a Jewish community of some importance. There was also a school of philosophy. The christian community seems to have been formed of a cross-section of these elements and to have had just the troubles one might expect from such a heterogeneous grouping.

When Paul came to write this letter (or group of letters) his conversion to christianity was already some twenty years behind him. He had travelled and taught all over the north-eastern Mediterranean. But his fire, freshness and vigour are undiminished, and he is at the greatest period of his writing activity, sending to different churches on different occasions the four great letters which have been so formative for christian theology down the ages. To the stormy community of Corinth he is writing for the fourth time at least—two of the letters are lost. The Corinthians seem to have caused him constant worry since half-a-dozen years previously when he stayed there for eighteen months to work among them and preach to them, until he finally judged it wise to leave as a result of a squabble among the Jews. It is about the year 55 AD, and Paul is writing from Macedon in north Greece.

Book list

C. K. Barrett, *A commentary on the second epistle to the Corinthians* (1970).

K. Schelkle, *The second epistle to the Corinthians* (1969).

1

Establishing relationship
2 Cor 1:1–2:13

2 Cor 1:1–2. Address and greeting

Paul begins his letter with the formal greeting customary
in letters of the period; this greeting is comparatively
short, for he has written to them before and fairly recently. Three points deserve notice. The letter is addressed to 'the church of God which is at Corinth': there
is a delicate interplay between the total independent
value of each assembly of christians in its own place—
each is the church of God and in this sense self-sufficient
—and the organic connection between communities by
which all form the one body of Christ. It is also addressed
to 'the saints' in the whole of Achaia: the members of the
church make up the holy assembly corresponding in the
new dispensation to the holy people which God founded
for himself at the exodus; the christian's vocation is to
be holy, to participate in the holiness of God, to be
marked off by this vocation. Thirdly, Paul wishes them
'peace'; this is the normal Jewish greeting even today,
but for the christian it takes on new dimensions, as being
the peace of Christ, which becomes almost *the* characteristic par excellence of the christian.

*1. How independent should the local church com-
munity be?*

2. *In what sense is the christian separate from the world?*

3. *How is 'peace' distinguishable from spinelessness in the face of evil?*

2 Cor 1:3–11. Comfort in persecution

There is no Anglo-Saxon reticence about Paul: he speaks freely about his emotions and tribulations, understating neither his sorrows nor his triumphs. A theology of christian suffering is one of the chief riches of this letter. The suffering which Paul had to undergo in Asia is unknown: was it an illness such as he had in Galatia (Gal 4:14)? This is suggested by his remark 'we were carrying our own death warrant with us' (1:9). Or was it a persecution akin to his 'fighting the wild animals at Ephesus' (1 Cor 15:32)? We know very little about the three years Paul spent at Ephesus, at the end of which he wrote this letter, and he may well have been imprisoned and threatened with death. In any case the suffering brings him to reflect on his two-way connections within the body of Christ: in his suffering Paul is united both to Christ and to his fellow christians. When he suffers it is the sufferings of Christ which overflow to him (1:5), and he in some way in his own body 'completes what was lacking in the sufferings of Christ' (Col 1:24). The christian is, even physically, not just in some vague spiritual way, the extension of Christ's body, so that when he suffers Christ suffers, and his sufferings too are redemptive.

This idea is one of the most basic of all in Paul's thought, and he holds it with an astounding realism which makes such expressions as 'the *mystical* body' wholly inadequate. It is not a mere metaphor like the

classic figure, already then familiar in literature, for a
'body politic' or 'corporation'. The most striking example
of his realism is in 1 Cor 6 : 12–20 when he teaches that
the horror of a christian giving himself to a prostitute is
that he is taking Christ's body and uniting it to the
whore; this can only be if we are physically part of Christ.
But it is not merely physical, for by baptism we take on
as our own Christ's history; his crucifixion and resurrection are ours, we have undergone them in Christ. J. A.
T. Robinson expresses it forcefully (*The Body*, p 63) :
'new tissues take on the rhythms and metabolism of the
body into which they have been grafted' : so, as we share
Christ's being, his actions are ours and our actions are
his. And the same communication as between Christ and
the christian exists between fellow-christians; such is the
reality of the bond. So for Paul's fellow-christians his
sufferings, redemptive in Christ, bring strength to bear
their sufferings; this is Paul's meaning rather than the
somewhat weak 'consolation'; in other contexts the word
indicates the strength to persevere (Rom 15 : 5), and here
too it enables them to bear suffering in firm hope and
reliance on God.

*1. How can we take literally that we are limbs of
Christ's body?*

*2. What is the point of suffering for a christian? Should
a christian deliberately inflict suffering on himself?*

*3. Is Paul being sentimental in this passage? Or
boastful?*

2 Cor 1 : 12–2 : 13. Paul's change of plans

Paul now sets out to give an explanation of his failure to
fulfil a promise. The explanation is striking in two ways,

firstly because Paul takes such trouble to explain, and secondly because of his reasoning about Christ as the Amen of the Father. The Corinthians were not the model among the communities founded by Paul, which makes his patient explanation all the more remarkable. Already the first epistle he wrote to them reflected discord in the community. Then, after a visit to Corinth during which he promised to return, he sent an envoy in his stead, who was insulted in such a way that Paul was compelled to rebuke them sharply by letter. This letter, now lost, whose severity clearly continued to worry Paul, must have had an effect, for next Titus brought the news (7 : 6) that they were repentant and again well-disposed towards Paul. It is a mark of Paul's patience that after so much cantankerousness on their part he still spells out the explanation that the change of plans with which they rebuke him was motivated entirely by concern for their interests. Paul's obviously excitable temperament makes it the more extraordinary that only once in his letters does he seem to lose patience, when he calls the Galatians 'idiotic' (Gal 3 : 1).

Paul's reasoning is not immediately clear: he does not make emphatic assertions ('yes, yes') and denials ('no, no') at the same time, as though at random or contradicting himself. This would be directly contrary to the christian message, for there is no shadow of untruth in Christ. On the contrary, Christ is himself the truth and fidelity of the Father. The argument is founded on a Hebrew pun—an interesting piece of evidence that Paul, though writing in Greek and using the Greek bible, in fact thought in Hebrew or Aramaic. In Hebrew 'amen' has a double meaning; firstly it means 'so be it' or 'yes', a formula of acceptance and agreement. But it also has the sense of confirmation, firmness, stability, fidelity, and in this sense is used particularly of God's word which is reliable because of his unshakeable fidelity. The basis, therefore, of Paul's thought is that his word must be reliable because Christ is the amen of the Father, the final 'yes' of God to his promises, the proof and fulfilment of his faithfulness. Contained already in the message of the old testament, he is also its culmination and completion. Possibly also when Paul calls Christ the amen he is thinking of the amen to the prayers of the liturgy, for 1 Cor 14 : 16 shows that amen was already used at least in the great eucharistic prayer; we, in the person of Christ, say the amen, which represents Christ, to the prayer to the Father.

In 1 : 21–22 Paul makes one of his rare allusions to the Trinity, inexplicit but full of meaning. His approach to the Trinity is always strictly functional; he is not interested in the abstract interrelationship of the three persons but sees them in terms of their dynamic individual relationships towards ourselves. God, by which Paul means the Father, is the author of our relationship to Christ; it is he who seals and anoints us (probably a reference to baptism, which is often called a sealing in the early church) implanting us in Christ. The guarantee of this relationship to Christ is the Spirit, given to us as a pledge or first payment—Eph 1 : 14 calls it the pledge of our inheritance—which means that our inheritance is already a reality, though it has yet to be completed. It is perhaps particularly to the Corinthians that Paul speaks of the Spirit, for there the curious ecstatic phenomena associated with the Spirit were most obvious (1 Cor 12–14). Yet, more important than these 'pentecostal' happenings, the Spirit gives also understanding of the knowledge of

God, by the affinity to God which it gives (1 Cor 2 : 10–16; Gal 4 : 6). It is the Spirit which works the transformation in us, making us members of Christ and so sons of the Father.

1. Of what interest is it to us, what does it add to our understanding of Jesus, to know that he is the fulfilment of the old testament promises?

2. What difference is made by the Spirit to our relationship with God? Who has this relationship?

3. Can we understand anything about the interrelationship of the persons in the Trinity? Is there any point in trying?

2

The apostolate and the problem of death
2 Cor 2:14–5:10

2 Cor 2:14–3:3. The work of the apostolate

With one of his characteristic leaps of thought—perhaps a new start after a pause in dictation—Paul turns from the difficulties of his relations with the Corinthians in particular to the happiness of the work of the apostle in general. First he uses two figures to characterise the work of the apostolate. The apostle is put into Christ's triumphal procession by God; after a great victory a general would display his captives and booty in a procession culminating in a final sacrifice; the meaning is that christians are part of the triumphal display which Christ presents when he 'hands over the kingdom to God the Father' (1 Cor 15:24), but there is no clear thought whether they are captives or soldiers in the procession. The figure of the christian as the smell of Christ is perhaps best explained by reference to the old testament idea of the sweet smell of sacrifice; it is christians who constitute and who spread the noticeable effects of Christ's sacrifice. The smell of animal sacrifices provides an excellent image of the two possible effects of Christ, for the presence of Christ occasions a judgement: for some he is a foundation-stone, for others a stumbling-block, depend-

63

ing on the reaction to him, whether he is accepted or rejected.

1. In what sense are christians Christ's captives, or is this a misleading image?

2. How can Christ be a 'smell of death that leads to death'?

3. Is Paul too possessive in his attitude to the Corinthians?

2 Cor 3:4–4:6. The glory of the apostolate

The nucleus of this passage is a comparison of the ministry of the new covenant with that of the old. Paul is led on by the mention of the letter of recommendation written on the hearts of the Corinthians to a digression on the glory of the two ministries, that of the new covenant, written on men's hearts and bringing life, contrasted with that of the old, engraved on stone and bringing death. This contrast is prepared by the promise made by Jeremiah and Ezekiel of a new covenant which will not depend on old and hard-and-fast institutions but on the conscience of the individual, on the direct communication of God to the individual in the Spirit. After the death of the institutions of Israel by the exile, when temple and monarchy were destroyed, the nation was to come to life again by the Spirit of God being breathed into the dead bones; thus the Spirit is associated with life and vitality. For Paul the Spirit is also essentially a spirit of freedom (3:17), freedom from bondage to the old law and its rigidity. And throughout the new testament it is the possession of the Spirit which defines and marks out a christian. It brings freedom from the hopeless situation of attempting to fulfil the demands of the law, allowing man to acknowledge his own weakness and need for Christ, drawn to serve only by the works of love. It is hard to visualise the sense of freedom and of lightening of a burden experienced by one who emerged into the calm and warm freedom of Christ after an unbending slavery to the law.

Another means here used by Paul to contrast the two covenants relies on a rabbinic-style exegesis of the passage in Exodus where Moses' face is said to have shone so much after his encounter with God that he had to wear a veil. Light is a symbol of the awesome presence of God —it has been said that the Hebrew attitude to God in some ways resembled an attitude towards high tension electricity—the burning light of Palestine can be fierce and terrible as well as bringing warmth and life; it is also mysterious, present yet distant, all-pervading yet impossible to possess. The qualities of light, combined with Israel's soul-shaking experience of the appearance of God in lightning on Mount Sinai, brought it about that the unspeakable and terrifying glory of God was conceived in these terms.

Paul's message is, then, that the glory of the old revelation was not so bright, was not so complete a revelation of God's nature as that in Christ, and anyway the Jews refuse to look at the fullness of revelation in Christ. But we who accept the light are ourselves lit up and transformed by it until we ourselves become the light of God's glory. This is his powerful way of expressing the transformation of the christian into Christ. It is, however, a gradual process; writing to the Galatians (4 : 19) Paul compares it to the forming of the foetus in the womb. First we are the mirrors and then we are the image itself.

These are metaphors used already in the old testament to show the identity but separateness of wisdom with God; to the Greek-trained mind even more than to us they express identity, for the Greeks concentrated on the formal identity of reflection and thing reflected, neglecting the difference in matter. Paul is thus saying in as vivid a way as possible that though the christian retains his separate identity he nevertheless shares in and is permeated by the divinity which is in Christ.

A further point, made in 4:2, is worth noting: Paul's principles on teaching. He is aware that he has the authority of Christ, but he never in fact 'commands'. He comes very close to it twice (1 Cor 5:12–13 and 11:16), but his conviction is that the truth should be self-authenticating, so that the clarity of the truth is recognisable 'to every human being with a conscience'. This is why he always explains the theological principles on which his practical decisions are founded—the explanations which have made his letters not ephemeral directives but permanent bases of christian theology. But his approach is not a cold and logical exposition, to be taken or left; he does not hesitate to exhort and persuade his brothers, and to show the warmth of his affection.

1. 'The dispensation of death, carved in letters on stone.' Isn't this an extreme way, even for a christian, to refer to the ten commandments? Have they really 'no splendour at all'?

2. Think of another, modern image corresponding to Paul's metaphor of mirrors and light to express sameness and separateness.

3. If the light of God is directly revealed to us, how can we need the church as a teacher?

2 Cor 4:7–5:10. The prospect of death

It is part of the vitality and immediacy of Paul's letters that we can see his thought developing; we see the birth of Paul's hope in a personal and individual union with the Lord after death.

From the beginning of the passage the thought of death predominates. Whether as a result of his persecutions, or of his age or his illness, Paul is confronted with the thought of approaching death. Because of his hope in the resurrection he is, however, undismayed, and in the first paragraph contrasts the power of the life of the risen Christ in himself with his own weakness unaided, alluding at the end—'so death is at work in us but life in you'—to the theme of the redemptive value for others of his own sufferings.

It is after this that the evolution takes place in Paul's thought.

The earliest christian hope had been dominated by the expectation of the second coming of Christ and the general resurrection of the dead to meet him and join him in his triumphal procession (see under 2:14–3:3). This second coming was imagined as accompanied by all the cataclysmic phenomena of the traditional end of the world, stars falling from heaven and great distress. The imagery was adopted wholesale from Jewish apocalyptic writings about the coming of the messiah at the end of time, and the event was expected to occur very soon. But when it continued to delay, this form of the hope dimmed and it began to be seen that the important second coming was the coming of Christ's spirit at Pentecost and that the reign of Christ began at his resurrection (the full development of these are seen respectively in the gospel of John and in the letters to the Ephesians and Colossians). It was, however, still not clear—it is not clear today—how much of the imaginative picture of the triumphant second coming on the clouds is merely imagery which must be interpreted, and how much is to be taken literally. The falling stars and the chariot of clouds are, surely, figurative, but is the whole picture of a general last judgement? Or is there only an individual confrontation with Christ at death which has been generalised and dramatised in Matthew 25 : 31–46?

Whatever the truth of this, in the earlier letters to the Thessalonians and in 1 Corinthians the return of Christ in a triumphal procession had been the kernel of the hope for the dead. It is the foundation of Paul's thought in this passage until 5 : 5. Contemplating his own death, Paul's thought strains ahead to this triumphal procession, but he shudders at the idea that there may be a gap between his death and the general resurrection, so that his soul will be left for a time 'naked'. He accepts the terminology of the Greek philosophers by which at death the soul is separated from the body and left 'naked', but is too much of a semite to share their conception that the soul is at last liberated from the hampering toils of the body. According to Greek ideas, at death the soul, which is the only really important part of man, is set free from the 'tomb' of the body, which was nothing but an incubus. According to the sounder semitic anthropology, man is a whole, and the soul, far from being freed by the disintegration of the body, is left temporarily in a curious limbo—a form, but not the form of anything, like the smile of the Cheshire cat after the Cheshire cat has disappeared—which Paul dreads. He longs to put on the full immortality of the risen body without any such interim period.

Then suddenly at 5:6 Paul changes course and becomes full of confidence in the face of an early death, positively longing for it, because he sees that it means union with Christ. Paul had already seen that putting on the risen Christ in this life meant union with him, but this is the first glimpse of what now becomes—as his death becomes an ever more pressing reality—a stable acquisition: that this personal union persists even after death. To the ancient Hebrews death had meant exile and separation from God in a shadowy existence; then came the expectation of a general resurrection of the just at the last day; now, under the influence of the Greek idea of going off to join the immortal gods and heroes (Paul uses language associated with such ideas), the gap is filled with what is the logical consequence of the union of the christian to Christ. So in Philippians, not long after, he can write 'Life to me, of course, is Christ, but then death would bring me something more. . . I want to be gone and be with Christ' (1:21, 23) for he sees now that death means the completion of union to Christ.

1. What is the christian attitude to death? Should the christian positively long for death?

2. What is the condition of the soul between death and the resurrection of the body? What can the resurrection of the body be (cf 1 Cor : 15)? Do I exist in the interim period?

3. If Paul adopted pagan ideas can this still be called the christian revelation? Are they too revealed? Does Paul adulterate the tradition?

3

The work of Christ
2 Cor 5:11–6:13

2 Cor 5:11–19. God's reconciliation

This section is full of statements about redemption: Paul is led on to them as reasons for what might seem boasting for, he claims, God's work of redemption is so dazzling that one inevitably makes wild statements: 'the love of Christ overwhelms us'. There are several puzzling remarks, which we shall discuss in the reverse order of their occurrence in the passage:

(a) 'For our sake God made the sinless one into sin' (5 : 21). This expression has been at the root of explanations of Christ's work on the cross which centre on ideas such as that God vented his wrath against sin by plunging his knife into the heart of Christ, that Jesus on the cross suffered the pains of the damned and so expiated them for our sake, and so on. These theories which were so influential on medieval spirituality are founded simply on the failure to recognise a technical expression of old testament Greek, for it means 'made the sinless one *a sacrifice for* sin'.

But perhaps this is still bad enough, for it still uses the primitive language of bloody animal sacrifice. Certainly the new testament authors were quite prepared to use this language: the letter to the Hebrews contrasts the

71

efficacy of Christ's blood with the inefficacy of animal
blood. But both in that letter and in Paul it is only the
language of blood sacrifices which is used; it is not the
mere shedding of blood which redeemed us. Both authors
are quite clear that it is Christ's obedience, the expression
of his love, that is the crucial factor. This is not so clear
in our passage, except that the work of 'reconciliation'
should be expected to undo the work of separation; that
had been effected by Adam's disobedience, so should be
undone by the obedience of Christ, the second Adam.
This in fact is how Paul puts it when he is treating fully
(rather than, as here, by allusion only) of the reconciliation, writing to the Romans 'as by one man's disobedience many were made sinners, so by one man's obedience
many will be made righteous' (5:19). The sin and the
reparation are complementary. Similarly the letter to the
Hebrews is almost the document of Christ's obedience :
he 'learnt to obey . . . and having been made perfect . . .'
(Heb 5:8–9, cf 10:1–8).

So, as might be expected, the climax of the reconciliation was not a moment of rupture between Father and
Son in hate and anger, but was a climax of union in
obedience and love. It was precisely because of and in
this union between man and God that all men were
united or reconciled to God.

  *1. In view of this, is the whole idea of sacrifice still
abhorrent? What would you substitute?*
  2. Can one in any sense speak of God's anger?

(*b*) 'For anyone who is in Christ there is a new creation'
(5:17). The idea of a new creation of redeemed humanity in Christ is a consequence of the idea of Christ as a
new Adam : as Adam was the founder of the human race

(or, perhaps one should say, as Adam *stands for* the human race in the poetico-theological account of the fall) so Christ who reversed this work is the founder of a new human race. But does this amount to a whole new creation? In Jewish thought at the time of Paul, Adam is thought of as including within himself not merely humanity but all creation; he has become a sort of mythical figure of vast proportions and limitless potentiality; in his fall is implicated the whole of creation; it is a universal catastrophe. So according to these ideas the reversal of this catastrophe renews the whole world and can be called a new creation. It is this which gives Christ as man his pre-eminent position in the universe, making him, so to speak, the keystone. Paul will elaborate on this, in answer to the denial of Christ's status, when he writes to the Colossians: 'he holds all things in unity . . . As he is the beginning he was first to be born from the dead so that he should be first in every way' (Col 1 : 17–18).

This vision of Christ's universal pre-eminence may seem to depend entirely on the antitype, on the Jewish mythical figure of Adam, with whom Christ is contrasted. But it is possible to express the same thoughts without relying on this myth. If man is the summit of creation, whose relationship to God gives sense to the whole of creation, then Christ, who is both the perfect man and the man through whom this relationship to God is finally established, is the keystone of creation. Or, to borrow language from Teilhard de Chardin, the goal of the universe is evolution into the Omega-point; in this evolution Christ plays an irreplaceable role and marks the significant transition into the last stage of evolution. In this sense Paul means that there is a new creation in Christ, and for anyone who is in Christ.

1. Is it possible to express Christ's position in the universe without recourse to some myth or other? Have the Teilhardian myths any advantage over the scriptural ones?

2. Is the animal kingdom and nature as a whole involved in the fall and the redemption?

(c) 'Even if we did once know Christ in the flesh, that is not how we know him now' (5:16). This seems to deny the value of having seen Christ on earth, and indeed it is one of the striking things about Paul's letters—in comparison to almost all other christian literature—what scant use he makes of the stories of Jesus' life. This has given rise to the claim that for Paul the historical Jesus, even his death, are irrelevant.

The context of the remark is certainly controversy. From the first letter to the Corinthians we know that there were groups at Corinth divided among themselves, and one of them seems to have called themselves Peter's or Cephas' men (Cephas is the Aramaic form of Peter). Later on in this second letter Paul engages in controversy with people he sarcastically calls 'arch-apostles' (12:11) who are Hebrews and Israelites (11:22). All this suggests that his opponents at Corinth, who seem to be demanding his credentials as an apostle, are people who came from Palestine, perhaps with Peter on his way through to Rome, and had known Jesus during his earthly ministry. Perhaps they had been among the larger circle of disciples who were not numbered among the twelve.

To these Paul replies—the Jerusalem Bible translation is misleading—that knowledge according to the flesh has no claim (the phrase 'in the flesh' or 'according to the standards of the flesh' goes, as in the first part of the verse, with the *knowing*, not with *Christ*). He is making a contrast not between the historic and the risen Christ but between unenlightened knowledge and knowledge enlightened by the Spirit. Before the coming of the Spirit the apostles themselves had failed again and again to understand the message of Christ, and Paul hints that his opponents are limited to this sort of knowledge and still lack the full understanding provided by the Spirit in the new creation.

1. By what right can Paul tell that his interpretation is in the Spirit and theirs is according to the flesh?

2. How important, and why, is knowledge of the historical Jesus?

2 Cor 5:20–6:10. The hardships of an apostle

Paul returns again, not for the last time in this letter, to the subject of his sufferings. Here he links them explicitly to his vocation as Christ's ambassador; his acceptance of them proves that he is a servant of God (6:4), and he seems finally almost to glory in being misunderstood and misrepresented. Is this a subtle form of masochism?

In common with all new testament writers Paul conceives the work of an apostle as a service. The term 'ministry' has become so well-worn that we no longer realise what a reversal it was that leaders in the christian community should designate themselves as servants or slaves —the lowest and most despised class—instead of by titles which authorities in the ancient world normally used. They use no title associated with power, rulers, leaders, honour, but from the first it is a 'service' to which the seven 'deacons' (=servants) are elected in Acts 6:1–6.

Paul calls himself not only a slave of Christ but, earlier in this letter (4 : 5), a slave to the Corinthians.

But for Paul there is a special thought behind it : he assimilates his office of apostle with that of the suffering servant of the Lord in Isaiah. It was in terms of these prophecies that Jesus himself had seen his mission of suffering and humiliation : the servant voluntarily undergoes unjustified torture and public shame for the sins of others and by this means brings many to salvation (Is 52 : 13–53 : 12). Paul, as the servant of Christ, sees himself fulfilling the same pattern, and seems therefore to expect contempt and shame, 'prepared for honour or disgrace, for blame or praise' (6 : 8), and supremely indifferent to the good opinion of men (1 Cor 4 : 3–4). This is also why his sufferings complete the measure of Christ's, why he can say later 'we are weak as he was, but we shall live with him through the power of God' (2 Cor : 13.4). He sees it as the lot of the apostle to achieve his mission only through suffering and contempt after the pattern of his master.

1. Of what kind should the authority of a christian minister be? Is he a slave? Is his dignity compatible with this title?

2. Must the apostle suffer if he is to get anywhere? Must all christians?

3. Should a christian seek suffering?

4

Interlude
2 Cor 6:14–9:15

2 Cor 6:14–7:1. A warning against unbelievers

This is a curious isolated fragment which seems to have nothing to do with the passages on either side of it. If it is omitted and the letter read with a jump from 6:13 to 7:2, it makes just as good, if not better, sense. So it has been suggested that it could be the fragment of another letter inserted somewhat ineptly here. Is it by Paul? It is very carefully structured in a way not characteristic of his impetuous style: an initial statement built on a biblical allusion on not harnessing uneven oxen together, followed by five examples of impossible pairings and then four scriptural quotations. And there are a number of words which occur either nowhere else in the new testament or at least never elsewhere in Paul. There is also a striking similarity in ideas and expression to the Dead Sea scrolls from Qumran: they were a closed community always concerned to preserve themselves from contamination by outsiders, they use the antithesis light-darkness frequently (as does John), they alone at this date mention Belial as a person, and they call their community the temple of God—all characteristics of this passage. Who wrote it and how it penetrated here have not yet been satisfactorily explained.

Problematic to us is its separatism. 1 Cor 5:9–11 had

said explicitly that christians were not to withdraw from association with unbelievers, even if they were sexually immoral or usurers or swindlers. But now association, or at any rate teamwork, is forbidden with all unbelievers. It must simply be that the author of this fragment is more cautious than Paul. We know from Acts and Galatians that Paul's views on associating with non-Jews were not popular with some, notably the followers of James, bishop of Jerusalem, and that controversy over this flared up. Perhaps most instructive about this matter is that there could be controversy over such an important point of behaviour in the early church (each party concentrating on different ones among the many theological implications) and that both solutions should find a place in the inspired scriptures of the church.

The expression 'temple of God' used of the christian community does have pauline links. The Qumran community claims to be the temple of the living God to underline their opposition to the actual temple at Jerusalem which they considered to have been profaned. In christian thought the idea perhaps goes back to Jesus' promise, 'Destroy this temple and in three days I will raise it up', speaking of the temple of his body (Jn 2:19–21). In 1 Cor 3:16 and Eph 2:20–22 Paul speaks of the christian community as being the temple of God because it is Christ's body and the Spirit of God dwells in it. Elsewhere he speaks of the Spirit dwelling in individuals, but here it is the community, the local church, as a whole. This is the reason why each local church is treated by Paul as being of independent value, each complete in itself, 'the church of God which is at . . .', each able to judge and make its own decision.

1. On what sort of fundamental questions can christians disagree and to what extent?

2. Do we act as though we believed that each local community was the temple of God? Would any changes in church organisation be required if we did?

2 Cor 7:2–16. Learning by mistakes

The delicacy of Paul's sometimes stormy relations with the Corinthians is fully visible here. He begins to defend himself again with 'we have not injured anyone, or ruined anyone or exploited anyone'—can one see here a link with that readiest of charges in 8:20, maladministration of funds?—but checks himself to protest his affection for them. He presumably realises that they were still sensitive after the letter which distressed and chastened them so much (for the sequence of events, see explanations under 1:12–2.13), and could not take any more correction. So instead Paul encourages them with some words to help them realise how much they have learnt from the painful experience and to protest his solidarity with them in the pain he had to cause them. The letter must have been a masterpiece of tact, for in spite of its severity it seems actually to have increased their affection for him.

1. 'Fraternal correction is the highest form of charity.' Is it? What qualities should it have to be so?

2. Do you think Paul is here painting the picture rosier than it in fact was? Would this be justifiable?

2 Cor 8–9. The collection for Jerusalem

Paul now goes on to quite another matter, which occupies
the next two chapters. The background situation is two-
fold. We know from other sources that Jerusalem was
very hard hit by a famine in the late 40's of the first
century. There was scarcity of food throughout the Mediterranean world, but Palestine was particularly affected.
In addition there were in Jerusalem a number of old
people who had retired to spend the evening of their
days in the holy city and who lived almost wholly on
the charity of the pilgrims who came up for the feasts;
there were a number of them in the christian community,
for very early on the cry had been raised that they were
not all being treated alike (Acts 6:1). So there was in the
church at Jerusalem considerable poverty and need.

But there is another side to the matter. As we have
already seen, the Jerusalem community was none too
happy about the large numbers of non-Jews whom Paul
was bringing into the church. They had indeed granted
that the church should be open to gentiles (Acts 11:1–18)
but the underlying friction between them and Paul as
champion of the gentile church is clear enough (Acts 21:
22–25). Paul's plan was therefore to make a collection
among the large and, in part, comparatively prosperous
christian communities of Greece, which would supply
the very real needs of the community at Jerusalem, and
at the same time demonstrate their loyalty and consideration for the mother-church from which the faith
emanated.

There is, however, a literary problem about these two
chapters, which may cast interesting light on the whole
epistle and on the collection of Paul's letters in general.

Some evidence suggests that chapters 8 and 9 form an independent letter, and that chapters 10 to 13 form a third letter, so that 2 Corinthians is really a collection of letters. It may even be that chapters 8 and 9 are two independent letters, the former written to Corinth (there are a number of links with 1 Corinthians), and the latter a circular letter sent to all the churches of Achaia—ie Southern Greece—including Corinth. For the epistle to the Philippians a similar history has been suggested, that it is in fact a collection of three or four notes sent separately by the apostle. For the understanding of the text these questions—and they remain only questions, for no conclusive decision seems possible—are not of great importance. But it does enable us to form some idea of the frequency and informality of communication between Paul and his communities: he simply wrote to them when opportunity arose, rather than sitting down to compose an inspired epistle. And they on their side kept and treasured these notes, appreciating their importance, and collected them together when, in the early second century, the collection of Paul's correspondence was made up. From such chance glimpses must our picture of the very early church be built up.

The machinery of the collection seems to have been that the Corinthians first showed their willingness to contribute (8:10); perhaps they even suggested the collection. In his first letter (1 Cor 16:2) Paul had suggested 'every Sunday each one of you must put aside what he can afford', and had promised to send the collection up to Jerusalem by the hand of their chosen delegates, going himself if it turned out to be a worthwhile sum. In fact Paul's visit to Jerusalem in Acts 21 may have been with the proceeds, though there is no explicit

mention of handing over the money. However by the
time this present chapter was written the idea of the collection had spread to Macedonia, and Paul has definitely
undertaken to collect the money set aside, in company
with a delegate 'elected by the churches' (8 : 19). The
only trouble is that Paul is obviously extremely anxious
that the good intentions which started off the collection
may not have been very generously carried out.

It is striking that in his pleas Paul makes only the
barest of references to the 'needs of the saints' which
they are supplying (9 : 12). He makes no attempt, as
would a modern fund-raiser, to excite their pity for, or
interest in, the plight of the recipients. His chief concern
is the reaction of the Jerusalem community, concern that
they should be convinced by the collection that the
christians of Greece are good christians, and so 'give glory
to God' (9 : 13). But, apart from this, he looks at it entirely
from the point of view of the givers, that it is good to
give. The two motives he mentions are the imitation of
Christ's generosity in emptying himself and taking on the
condition of a servant (8 : 9, cf Phil 2 : 6–7), and the confidence in God's reward (9 : 6–11).

*1. Is Paul's obvious flattery of his correspondents a
legitimate means of encouraging their generosity? Is the
spirit of competition which he introduces too base a
motive?*

*2. Should the way the early church lived be of any
interest to those of us who are not historians?*

5

Paul the apostle
2 Cor 10:1–13:14

2 Cor 10:1–11. Paul asserts himself

There is no particular reason for thinking that these last
four chapters of the epistle are part of the same letter as
the first seven, if indeed the section on the collection is a
separate letter or letters. The violent tone is certainly at
variance with the gentle and conciliatory attitude, when
Paul is afraid to utter any criticism lest he open their
slowly healing wounds, in 7:2–16. But Paul did not
dictate his letters at a single sitting, and abrupt changes
of mood seem to have been typical of him, so this argument is not conclusive. In any case it is not important for
the understanding of these chapters.

Obviously a wholesale attack has been made on Paul's
claim to act as mentor of the community and this by
means of denigration of his character and talents as a
preacher. His opponents claim that they have more right
to guide than he, whence he calls them 'arch-apostles'
(cf comment (c) on 5:11–19). Paul admits that he is not
'a polished speechmaker' (11:16), so there must have been
something in this charge, but we are not therefore justified in accepting the legend that the 'thorn in the flesh'
mentioned in 12:7 was a stammer. It is perhaps frivolous
to recall the young man who fell asleep during one of
Paul's sermons and fell out of the window to his death

(Acts 20:7–12). If one may surmise from his letters Paul was certainly excitable, and perhaps got so carried away that his coherence and the consecutive development of his theme suffered. But he is also capable of passages of magnificent rhetoric (eg 6:3–10) and graphic description (eg 11:21–12:6).

But Paul's defence is not on grounds of eloquence, it is firstly that his authority has been given him by Christ. He does not explain when the grant of authority occurred, but two possible occasions come to mind, either at the moment of his conversion, in which case the authority came from Christ without any intermediary, or when this commission to preach to the gentiles was officially recognised by the church (Gal 2:7–8). More interesting is Paul's concept of his authority: both times that he mentions it (10:8 and 13:10), although each is in a threatening context, he stresses that the purpose of it is 'for building you up and not for pulling you down', using a little phrase from the story of the vocation of the prophet Jeremiah. Even at the height of his polemic he remains aware that his authority is not for his own dignity but as a service to them. It is against the background of this conviction that one must see the intention 'to punish any disobedience' (10:6). The idea of actually punishing is startling in a religious context—admonition and warning, perhaps, but what can only be some kind of temporal punishment hardly accords with our ideas of Christian freedom. Is it not of the essence of religious obedience that it be willing and not forced? And yet there is a case in 1 Corinthians of such a punishment actually taking place: exclusion from the community (5:1–13); and there it is conceived both as remedial for the offender and as a protection for the rest of the community.

1. Has punishment any place within the religious community? Why is the situation different from the secular sphere? If so, what sort of punishment and when?

2. Does Paul's tone of voice here square well with the gentleness of Christ?

3. To what extent can any preacher claim 'complete obedience'?

2 Cor 10:12–11:15. Paul defends himself by his zeal in his mission

The first paragraph (10:12–18) is somewhat obscure, but Paul is claiming that in exerting his influence over the Corinthians he is not pushing himself beyond the limits which God has set for him (this is a paraphrase of 10:13b) because of his warrant as apostle of the gentiles: the same warrant will carry him yet further when he can be sure of the Corinthians. It is this warrant or 'commendation' from the Lord that he means in 10:18, which gives him, rather than his opponents, the right to teach the Corinthians.

He then goes on to protest his single-minded love for them, the devotion that led him to avoid being the slightest burden to them, and his zealous care to keep them faithful. All this is summed up in the phrase 'I arranged for you to marry Christ so that I might give you away as a chaste virgin to this one husband'. The expression 'chaste virgin' sounds a bit icy, but is really burning hot, for Paul is here alluding to the whole old testament revelation of the love of God for Israel and Israel's return.

In the prophets, especially Hosea, Yahweh is represented as the ardent lover who searches with burning passion, with the hot and unswerving love of a boy for a girl, the fiancée he has cherished from her youth. But she, Israel, is unconcerned and faithless, casually flirting with other lovers, while Yahweh seeks with undeviating patience to win her back to his heart. This story of the romance of God with Israel receives its highest expression in the Song of Songs, a series of originally secular love poems which are applied to God and Israel. Later on, writing to the Ephesians, Paul will compare Christ's love for the church to that of a husband for his wife; it was this love which led him to die for her and to cherish her still. Now he applies the figure of the fiancée, once used of Israel, to the church of Corinth; it had been his ardent desire to be able to 'give her away' at Christ's marriage feast with her virginity unbroken by infidelity. The same figure, the marriage feast of the Lamb, the celebration of his marriage to the church, is the image with which the new testament ends (Rev 21:9).

1. How usefully is God's love for men compared with human love in this way?

2. To what extent should the gospel be preached without a fee being taken for it? Are some modern forms of payment unacceptable?

2 Cor 11:16–33. Paul's apostolic labours are his warrant

In spite of his declaration that he will not compare himself with the 'arch-apostles' (10:12), as Paul warms to his subject he does so, thus giving us perhaps the liveliest biographical details of himself that we possess, much more informative than the polished and hagiographical portrait provided in Acts. It is an impressive record of hardship endured in the twenty-odd years of his mission.

One may wonder why he mentions his weakness; the reason for detailing his endurance seems clear enough. But in fact perhaps the mention of his weakness gives the clue to that too. He is not in fact boasting about his endurance, but is recurring again to the theme of the suffering servant (see under 5:20–6:10): it is not his hardihood but his suffering and especially his humiliation which prove that he is the servant of God and the chosen apostle; this is perhaps why he mentions first the man-inflicted punishments and imprisonments, which are more humiliating, and makes a climax of the rather ridiculous scene of the hamper.

2 Cor 12:1–18. The power of God at work in Paul's mission

Paul now cites two sharply contrasting evidences of God's power at work in himself. There are a number of occasions recorded in the Acts (9:11; 16:9; 22:17) and the letter to the Galatians (2:2) when Paul had visions and special revelations, but these were always to guide him in his work. This seems to be the only mention of such a mystical experience; it seems to be of a different order to the others, an experience of union with God, for this is what he stresses by underlining that he was in paradise and the third heaven (ie the heaven of heavens, heaven itself or the innermost heaven), and that what he heard was strictly incommunicable, not merely secret. It seems to be an experience of the mystics that, no matter how hard they try, they cannot translate into any medium of human communication, visual or aural, the experience of their meeting with God. This is the full meaning of 'things that no eye has seen and no ear has heard' (1 Cor 2:9); they are not simply secrets which may not be revealed, but they are of their nature beyond the grasp of our present imaginative and sensual media of communication. Paul certainly had extraordinary privileges of this order—he mentions casually elsewhere that he had the gift of tongues—but makes little play with them, precisely because of their incommunicability. Writing earlier to these same Corinthians (1 Cor 14:26–31) he had taught that such things must not be paraded but used only when this is for the common good, when they can be understood. On his own part he also shows a rather charming reticence at revealing this secret privilege he has kept so long hidden.

The culminating proof, however, of Paul's apostolic mission being from God is, paradoxically, his own weakness, so that his power *must* come from God. For this to have any value as a proof the 'thorn in the flesh' must have been something visible to all, or both thorn and the power which overcame it could have been inventions. Thus 'temptations of the flesh', ie sexual ones, would not do—nor would the presence of such temptations cut much ice to the inhabitants of a city which was notorious for all kinds of sexual immorality. It must have been something which was so well known to his correspondents that he need do no more than allude to it. Among the many suggestions (small stature, an impediment of speech) perhaps the most acceptable is that it was an unattractive and humiliating recurrent disease. He had such a disease in Galatia, writing years later 'you never showed the least sign of being revolted or disgusted by my disease that was such a trial to you' (Gal 4:14), which speaks volumes about the shame and distress it caused him. The expression used for 'beat' suggests recurrence (it really indicates a series of blows), and this may explain the mysterious allusions at the beginning of the letter (2 Cor 1:8–11).

What ever it was, it leads him to conclude his autobiographical defence with the supreme statement of acceptance and humility, 'it is when I am weak that I am strong'. For Paul one of the prime ideas associated with God and Christ is that of force and strength. The language of the cross is God's power to save, Christ is the power and wisdom of God (1 Cor 1.18, 24); at the resurrection what will take place is a transformation in power (1 Cor 15:43). Later he threatens to come to Corinth in the power of Christ (2 Cor 13:4). It is in fact not his own personal qualities but the proofs of the power of God at work in himself, signs, marvels, miracles (12:12), as well as the more individual and spectacular ones, that he has used throughout this passage to show his divine mission.

1. Has Paul simply been indulging in a disguised and subtle kind of boasting?

2. Should revelations to private persons play any part in our religious lives? Can 'pentecostal' phenomena be regarded as genuine?

3. Can we distinguish when we act in Christ's power and in our own?

2 Cor 12:19–13:10. A final warning
Paul concludes with a fairly energetic warning against the disorders which he clearly expects to find when he

comes to Corinth. It was a community where unity of heart would not come easily. An undercurrent of theological differences has been the background of much of the letter, but 1 Corinthians shows that there were social, economic and intellectual differences too: some were philosophers trained in Greek wisdom, others quite unsophisticated; some were rich, others poor; some were cautious ritualists terrified of contamination with paganism, others could see no harm in unrestricted contacts. When to these differences were added the difficulties created by the libertinism of Corinth on the one hand and charismatic gifts on the other, it is no wonder that there was a good deal of 'wrangling, backbiting' and the rest. The two chief areas of difficulty seem, from this passage, to have been in the field of personal relationships and sexual morality.

The way Paul questions them is noteworthy (13 : 5). Their examination of their conduct in these matters is itself the test whether they are 'in the faith' and whether Christ is really in them. There is no question of faith being simply a matter of accepting a body of teaching, a purely intellectual matter. Being in the faith must involve a whole way of life, allowing Jesus Christ to act in them in the framework of the christian way of life and the christian community.

1. To what extent does an un-christian environment excuse one?

2. Is it meaningful to speak of faith in the case of someone whose practice is entirely non-christian?

3. Can Paul really mean 'I shall have no mercy' (13 : 2)?

2 Cor 13:11–13. Final good wishes

The final blessing is tantalising, as one of the few hints about the Trinity in Paul. Although the Spirit is of prime importance throughout his writings, there is very little about his relationship to the Father and to Christ, and we have to rely on such hints as this where 'the Lord Jesus Christ', 'God' and 'the Holy Spirit' are obviously parallel to each other. What is abundantly clear in Paul is that by the Spirit the absent Christ is present, and the power of God; but one may wonder whether the Spirit is merely the spirit of Jesus or the indwelling of God. This is perhaps due to the difficulty of thinking of a spirit (the spirit of the age, the spirit of endeavour, the spirit of Christ) as a person. But then it is not much easier to think of God as a person, once one has exorcised the image of a bearded old man in the sky. When used of God the concept of person too is analogical, and obviously not to be assumed to correspond exactly to what we mean when speaking of a human person.

In any case the theology of the Spirit as a person is still only emergent in Paul, and is chiefly shown by the parallelism, here and elsewhere, between the three persons of the Trinity.

1. What can be meant by the Spirit as a person?

2. How important is an appreciation of the Trinity for life as a christian?

3. How demonstrative should liturgical greetings be— 'a holy kiss'?

Philippians

Jerome Murphy-O'Connor

Introduction

Paul's letters are never formal or stilted. The force of his personality always triumphed over both literary conventions and the intricacies of theological argument. But in Philippians the personal tone is more marked than in any other. This was because the community at Philippi (today Filibedjik in the north-eastern corner of Greece) was the only one that never gave him any trouble. Hence when writing to it Paul was always relaxed and at ease. The respect and loyalty accorded to him by the Philippians he repaid with trust. He writes as casually as he must normally have spoken, confident that he would be understood correctly. We are permitted to see the man as he really was, and not under the strain of a crisis as in the other letters. His serene composure almost obscures the fact that he was writing from a prison, probably in Ephesus (about 56–57 AD).

Paul's visit to Philippi is described at length in Acts 16:11–40. The Jewish community there must have been small and poor because they did not even have a synagogue; they prayed in the open air beside the river (16 : 13). The missionaries were hospitably received, but ran into difficulties with certain Roman citizens when Paul took away their source of revenue by curing a slave girl with a spirit of divination. They succeeded in having him flogged and thrown into prison for the night. This caused a situation which permits a revealing insight into Paul's character. The morning after, the jailer, on order of the magistrates, released the prisoners, and in a tone that can easily be imagined requested them to leave town (16 : 36). Standing square on his dignity Paul thereupon revealed his position as a Roman citizen, and demanded a rehabilitation as public as the condemnation. He was on sure ground, because the law strictly forbade the flogging of a Roman citizen, and the magistrates duly came and apologized. It would be a mistake to see this incident simply as a protest against an unjust and hasty legal decision. It was a shrewd strategic move to force at least a minimal degree of official recognition for the new religion.

Some time after his imprisonment in Ephesus Paul went back to Philippi for Easter (Acts 20 : 6), but throughout the six years that had elapsed since his first visit contact had been maintained. What appears in the new testament as 'The letter to the Philippians' in fact combines three letters written on different occasions. For the sake of convenience we shall term them A, B and C: *Letter A*: 1 : 1–2; 4 : 10–20; *Letter B*: 1 : 3–3 : 1; 4 : 2–9; *Letter C*: 3 : 2–4 : 1. These three letters were combined into the form of the present letter when another community, recognizing the universal value of Paul's teaching, asked the Philippians for copies of what the apostle had sent them. This was the beginning of the wider collection of writings that we now know as the new testament.

Book list

1. *Jerusalem Bible.* Useful for notes and marginal references, but the translation is too free to provide a basis for serious study.

2. *The Epistle to the Philippians* (in Black's *New Testament Commentaries*), F. W. Beare. Written for the Greekless student, this commentary is remarkable for the ease with which it combines profundity with clarity. It also contains a good annotated bibliography.

3. *Paul's Letters from Prison (Pelican New Testament Commentaries)* J. L. Houlden. A first-rate modern commentary on the RSV text, for Colossians, Philemon and Ephesians as well as Philippians.

1

Letter A
Phil 1:1–2; 4:10–2O

In this letter Paul thanks the Philippians for aiding him in his hour of need. He shows himself so deeply grateful that it is highly unlikely that this sentiment would not have betrayed itself earlier in the epistle. A close reading, however, brings to light only two possible allusions (1 : 5; 2 : 30) which are so vague and general as to lead us to suppose that the Philippians had already been thanked. Hence, we are forced to the conclusion that the epistle is not a literary unity, but a combination of originally distinct letters of which the earliest was letter A, the 'letter of gratitude'. This conclusion can be supported by a second argument. To suppose that what we term letter A was a part of the epistle carried by Epaphroditus on his return to Philippi is to assume that Paul delayed for several weeks to thank the Philippians, and did not avail of the services of the messengers who brought the news of Epaphroditus' illness from Paul's place of imprisonment to Philippi (2 : 26). Such an assumption is made improbable by the close bonds of friendship that bound the apostle to the Philippians. Letter A, therefore, is best understood as the letter sent by the apostle soon after receipt of the gift.

Phil 1:1–2

In their general lines the beginning of Paul's letters conform to the epistolary etiquette of his time. The name of the sender appears first, then that of the recipient(s), and finally a salutation: eg 'Claudius Lysias to His Excellency the governor Felix, greeting' (Acts 23:26). Despite their formal character the minute differences in the address of the various epistles permit us to catch a glimpse of Paul's mentality as he writes. In the two epistles that immediately preceded this one Paul introduces himself as an 'apostle' (1 Cor 1:1; Gal 1:1). The omission of any corresponding note here is therefore significant. Paul is not faced with a situation that obliged him to underline his authority. His letter is a sharing with friends.

Friendship, for Paul, involved love and respect, but fundamentally it was a matter of service. The title he here appropriates to himself and Timothy is 'slaves of Christ Jesus'. Paradoxically, this is a title of respect, because in the OT Moses, Abraham, David, and the prophets are termed 'slaves' of God. By reserving this title to himself and his immediate collaborators Paul manifests his awareness of being the successor of the great instruments of God of the OT. Yet the title is not personal but functional. Its dignity does not stem from the qualities of the bearer, but from the service into which he is incorporated. Christ himself 'took the form of a slave' (Phil 2:7), and it is in prolonging Christ's mission by bringing him to the Philippians that Paul performed the service that is the root of their relationship.

It is in responding to the call mediated by the apostle (cf Rom 1:7) that the Philippians have become 'saints'. The idea is not that they have automatically become 'holy', but that they have 'dedicated' themselves to a way of being which Paul characterises as 'in Christ Jesus'. This is basically a commitment to Jesus who is now Christ and Lord, but since Paul had already acquired the concept of the community as the body of Christ (Gal 2 : 26–29; 1 Cor 6 : 13–17; 10 : 14–21; 12 : 12–27) we cannot exclude the possibility that 'in Christ' also means 'in the whole Christ'. This mode of being Paul will qualify as a 'partnership' (Phil 1 : 5) and a 'fellowship' (Phil 3 : 10), because it is essentially a shared existence, as we shall see in more detail apropos of Phil 2 : 1 f. Dedication to God in Christ is manifested through mutual service within the community.

From among the saints Paul singles out 'the bishops and deacons' (RSV). Though materially correct, the apostle's meaning is obscured by this translation because in the first century 'bishop' and 'deacon' did not carry the connotations that are attached to these terms today. The JB rendering 'presiding elders and deacons' is better, but I am inclined to prefer the vaguer 'guardians and assistants'. As at Ephesus (Acts 20 : 17, 28), the senior members of the community supervised its affairs. How they were chosen and their exact role cannot be defined with accuracy. It seems probable that they are mentioned explicitly here because it was they who organized the aid given to the apostle.

Phil 4:10–23

It does not take great sensitivity to recognize an element of strain in this short note of gratitude. Two things are immediately remarkable. There is no direct expression of thanks, and the emphasis is on Paul's independence. Still

waters may run deep, but troubled waters tell us more.
Here we have no smooth flow, but jagged sentences in
which second-thoughts continually rear their heads. The
turbulent paragraph reveals a gracious, generous man,
easily touched by the thoughtfulness of others, but at the
same time conscious of a weighty responsibility.

He is overjoyed at the Philippians' gift. His wants have
been more than met (4:18). The interval (six years) had
been long since he had last received this sort of help
from them, and he looks back rather nostalgically to the
first days of the faith in Europe (4:15). Theirs was a real
partnership. Even in the difficult days in Thessalonica
(Acts 17:1–9) they found ways to send him money, and
not only once but twice. If they had not sent him anything in the meantime, it was not because of any lack of
good-will, but because they lacked the opportunity. This
may be an allusion to an economic set-back which de-
prived the community at Philippi of the means, but
Paul's mobility may also have been a factor.

Paul's joy at the reception of the gift was so intense
that its expression is broken up by interjections to ensure
that it will not be misunderstood. Although he firmly
defends the right of a minister to live by the gospel (1 Cor
9:3–14), he was desperately afraid in his own case that he
might be thought to preach for gain. His pride in the fact
that he earned his living by his own hands (1 Thess 2:9;
2 Thess. 3:8) had its roots in a deep-seated concern that
his true motive for preaching the gospel should not be
obscured. Even the suspicion of a tainted motive could be
sufficient to create an obstacle to the reception of the
gospel (1 Cor 9:12). This reveals the apostle's understanding of preaching as an activity that involved the
whole person. In his view there was a lot more to it than

purely verbal proclamation. The power of the word could be vitiated by the personality of the preacher. His totally disinterested dedication to Christ affords his words their only credibility.

The situation was further complicated at the time of writing of this letter. The collection for the poor of Jerusalem had just been inaugurated and Paul, by stipulating that he would not carry the money to Jerusalem personally, reveals himself to be fully aware that the collection was liable to give rise to accusations of self-aggrandisement (1 Cor 16:1–4). Whatever his need, the reception of a personal gift at just such a moment would inevitably cause a certain embarrassment.

It is against this background that Paul's stubborn stress on his independence must be understood. He claims to be entirely indifferent to circumstances, to be unmoved either by abundance or misery. At first sight this would appear to be a reflection of the stoic ideal expressed by Socrates in answer to the question who is the wealthiest, 'He that is content with least, for contentment is nature's wealth', but this stoic remoteness is entirely foreign to Paul. His detachment is conditioned by an overriding commitment to Christ (4:13). This absorbs him so completely that there is no room left in his make-up for preoccupation with the material circumstances in which he happens to find himself. No stoic could carry 'the daily pressure upon me of my anxiety for all the churches' (2 Cor 11:28). Nor could Paul were it not for the strength he draws from Christ. We can hardly be far wrong in seeing the concern of the Philippians as one of the channels of this grace.

The Philippians also benefit by their gift (4:17) which is described as 'a sweet fragrance (not as in RSV 'a fragrant offering'), a sacrifice acceptable and pleasing to God' (4 : 18). The use of this terminology drawn from the oт cult in Rom 12 : 1 and Eph 5 : 1–2 strongly suggests that Paul is thinking not so much of the gift in itself as of the Philippians' giving. Phil 2 : 17 which speaks of 'the sacrifice and liturgy that is your faith' confirms this interpretation. By thus spiritualizing cultic terminology Paul translates into reality the prophetic interpretation of God's will, 'I desire mercy, not sacrifice' (Hos 6 : 6 = Mt 9 : 13; 12 : 7). Loving concern, symbolised by the gift, is the true sacrifice, the one adequate expression of the believer's 'dedication' (cf Phil 1 : 2). Here we see the apostle's concern not to let religion degenerate into a series of external observances. The practical attitude of the Philippians no matter how mundane in appearances, is superior to any ritual sacrifice, because it is a loving participation in the trouble of another (4 : 14).

1. What justification can there be for considering a letter written out of a spirit of friendship and gratitude as normative for the church today?

2. How is independence to be reconciled with a willingness to receive from others?

3. How can purity of motive be translated into a way of life?

2

Letter B (first part)
Phil 1:3–2:1

It is equally possible that the address (1 : 1–2) belonged to
this letter. It was treated as pertaining to letter A more
for the sake of convenience than anything else. An editor
who worked with the intention of combining three letters
into one would naturally suppress two addresses and two
conclusions. The reasons for distinguishing this letter
from letter A have already been discussed. Hence we
have here only to note the fundamental features that
make it imperative to consider 3 : 2–4 : 1 a separate letter
(C). In this latter text Paul is obviously desperately worried that the insidious propaganda of judaeo-christian
missionaries might affect his cherished community at
Philippi. Nothing of this is to be perceived in letter B.
The community is not free of troubles (1 : 28), but these
come from their pagan fellow-citizens. In both letters,
therefore, there is an element of danger for the community, but in each case the source is different, and a similar
difference can be detected in the apostle's reaction. The
almost frantic concern of letter C is replaced by a calm
confidence in letter B.

Phil 1:3–11. Thanksgiving and prayer
With the exception of Galatians, an expression of gratitude is found immediately after the address in every ex-

tant pauline letter. It was part of the epistolary convention
of the time, and since its function was to introduce the
vital theme of the letter we may legitimately hope for
clues to Paul's mind even in this use of a conventional
form. When compared with other thanksgivings three
features here stand out as unique.

Firstly, Paul offers his prayer 'with joy' (1 : 4), an indication that his letter is not prompted by a serious problem within the community. The Philippians are not split
into factions as were the Corinthians, nor are they in
danger of being seduced from the faith as were the Galatians. It is easy to visualize Paul's relaxed frame of mind,
and the affection with which he contemplates this unique
community; a little later this escapes in the exclamation,
'How I yearn for you all with the affection of Christ
Jesus' (1 : 8).

This exclamation contains the second unique feature,
namely, the expression 'you all' which also appears in
1 : 4, and twice in 1 : 7. Paul makes no distinctions; all
are equal in his heart. Some commentators consider that
the emphasis on 'all' must be related to the frequent exhortations to unity that this letter contains (1 : 27; 2 : 2;
4 : 2). It is not necessary, however, to accept their inference that disputes and rivalries had become a major problem at Philippi. For Paul the life of faith was lived in
Christ, and he desired above all else that this unity in
commitment should be manifest on the level of practical
living. His repeated stress on the need for unity is related
not to a problem at Philippi but to his understanding of
the christian ideal; it is the tautology of earnestness, but
it clearly indicates the principal concern of the letter.

The third unique feature of this thanksgiving is Paul's
reference to a special feature of this unity in Christ,

namely, the 'partnership' (*koinōnia*) of Paul and the Philippians in the spread of the gospel (1 : 5, 7). The apostle's allusion to 'the first day', brings us back to the more explicit text of letter A (4 : 15–16) where, as we saw, it was a question of monetary assistance. In letter A we also noted the possibility of another form of assistance; the medium of God's strengthening grace is the loyalty and love of the Philippians (4 : 13) which enables Paul to struggle on despite all difficulties. The fortifying effect of example, though in the reverse direction, is mentioned by Paul in 1 : 14. It is in this perspective that the apostle here terms the Philippians 'co-sharers with me in grace' (1 : 7). This grace is directly related to 'the defence (*apologia*) and confirmation of the gospel'. The work of spreading the good news is a responsibility that falls not merely on those officially appointed to preach but on the whole community. Paul's commitment to the word of God became eloquent in the sufferings he was prepared to accept for the gospel. He expects precisely the same of the Philippians; 'with one mind striving side by side for the faith of the gospel and not frightened in anything by your opponents' (1 : 27–28). We shall consider this word-less but supremely effective form of witness in the context of 2 : 14–16, where Paul touches on it with somewhat greater detail. Enough has been said to show that the Philippians' partnership with the apostle was at a much deeper level than that of financial assistance.

Having justified his affection for the Philippians, the apostle specifies the object of his prayer. Ultimately, this is that they may stand 'pure and unfaltering' before their judge at the second coming of Christ, the day of the final judgement. The Greek word translated by 'pure' really means 'without foreign admixture', all of a piece.

In terms of his commitment to Christ the average believer is a mixture of loyalty and infidelity; as 'spirit' he is drawn in one direction, but as 'flesh' he follows a different orientation. If he does not dominate this tension he falters and stumbles. Hence Paul's prayer is that the Philippians may one day attain to absolute consistency of character, total commitment. Despite his love, the apostle was not so sanguine as to believe that they had already attained this ideal, and he was fully aware of the difficulties that the mixture of faith and non-faith, loyalty and infidelity, created for the moral judgement. This domain was important because the apostle continually emphasises that commitment is not a matter of thinking but of doing. Hence he also prays for the development of their moral insight (1 : 9). Only through realization in action does the original decision of faith gradually pervade the whole personality.

Life is so complex that every moral situation is in fact unique. The structure may be duplicated, but the components are never the same. Yet in each case the christian must choose 'what is excellent'. The Greek term means 'the things that really matter'. For Paul these are not spiritual realities, but the needs of others, because in his theology the question that the believer must ask himself when confronted with a moral decision is not 'Is this in accordance with the law?' but 'Will this make a positive contribution to the being-in-Christ of others?'. The answer to such a question inevitably involves elements which resist purely intellectual analysis. Hence, while Paul prays that the Philippians may have 'knowledge', he also prays that they may have 'discernment'. This latter term was first used in Greek medical texts to mean the capacity to make a correct judgement without rational criteria. As used by Paul it means an instinctive assessment of needs that cannot be rationalized. It is a sensitivity to what is most appropriate for each. The Jew felt that the law provided adequate guidance: 'you approve what is excellent because you are instructed in the law' (Rom 2 : 18). Paul disagreed completely. Sensitivity such as he required could never be learned from a system of precepts. It could only originate in love. Genuine love has an unmistakable impact. But while easy to recognize in others, it is not an entirely safe criterion of one's own personal activity, because of the danger of self-deception. The intensity of an impulse is no guarantee of its authenticity. This is why Paul prays for growth in love ('that your love may abound more and more'). Only the love of an adult in Christ (contrast 'babes in Christ', 1 Cor 3 : 1; cf 14 : 20) provides adequate insight in a moral situation, because that love has matured through a continued sharing which makes him utterly responsive to the demand of God expressed in the needs of the whole Christ.

1. In attempting to solve the problems posed by christian unity should priority be given to discussion or to practical cooperation?

2. What factors have led to the break-down of the close partnership between pastors and people that Paul describes? What can be done to revitalize the idea? What is the most important form such partnership should take?

3. What are the dangers inherent in stressing love as the guide to action in a situation which demands a moral decision? How can they be avoided?

Phil 1:12–26. News of Paul's condition and prospects

After the initial thanksgiving and prayer Paul's thoughts turn to his own situation which he knew would be a matter of concern to the Philippians. He is not at all sure what the outcome of his imprisonment will be. It could be the death sentence. But it is typical of his intense dedication that he speaks first of the effects of his imprisonment on the local church (1 : 12–18), and only then reflects on what it might mean for him personally (1 : 19–26).

Paul was detained in a 'praetorium' (1 : 13). This term was originally used to designate the general's tent in a military camp, but outside of Rome it was used of the official residence of a Roman governor. Thus the trial of Jesus before Pilate took place in the praetorium at Jerusalem (Jn 18 : 28 f), and that of Paul in the praetorium established in the palace of Herod at Caesarea (Acts 23 : 35 f). There was also a praetorium at Ephesus, because it was the seat of the proconsul of Asia to whom a cohort of the praetorian guard was assigned. Paul does not say why he was imprisoned, but the way in which 1 : 13 is formulated would seem to hint that it was on a pretext which has now been displaced by a general awareness that he has been made to suffer because of his commitment to Christ. In Jerusalem the accusation that Paul had violated one of the temple regulations was used to camouflage a deep-rooted hostility to his whole teaching (cf Acts 21 : 28; 24 : 6; 25 : 7–8). Something similar may well have happened at Ephesus; the tactic is common even today, eg the charge that a missionary is a commun-

ist is used as a counter to his plea for humanitarian treat-
ment of a native population.

The reaction of the members of the local community
to Paul's imprisonment was not uniform. A minority
began to walk very softly, obviously afraid of attracting
notice and becoming 'involved'. The majority, however,
found themselves strengthened. They did not hide, but
preached without fear. They took over the apostle's role,
but with a significant difference in motivation. Some felt
themselves inspired to continue the work. They felt themselves constrained to articulate verbally what Paul was
'saying' dramatically by his imprisonment (1 : 16). Others
found this imprisonment a perfect occasion for showing
Paul that the community could survive and develop
without him (1 : 17). In their small jealous minds they
hoped to add chagrin to his chains. Paul's reaction is an
eloquent shrug: 'So what! Christ is being preached, and
that is the one thing that matters', but the note of deter-
mination evident in 'yes, and I shall rejoice' reveals that
he was touched on the raw. Not because of the personal
affront, but because he must have had serious misgivings
about the value of a proclamation stemming from unworthy motives (cf letter A). It is against this background
that Paul's exhortations to unity in this letter are to be
read. Because of his actual experience he was afraid that
similar factions *might* develop within the Philippian
community.

Once begun Paul continues in a more personal strain.
'Deliverance' in 1 : 19 is not release from prison. The
Greek term used is elsewhere translated by 'salvation'.
Whatever the accusations of men he is confident of his
ultimate vindication by God. But he has misgivings about
his capacity to endure. If he struggles through it will be

due to the prayers of the Philippians and to the 'bounti-
ful supply' (not the banal 'help' of the RSV) of faith and
courage provided by the Holy Spirit. Knowing that he
can count on both, the apostle is suddenly confident that
he will not disgrace the gospel. The Greek conveys a note
of eagerness and enthusiasm that says much about what
the christian life should be. What matters to Paul is that
his existence be a manifestation of the compassion and
love of Christ, that Christ be made tangible in his person
in such a way as to command respect and admiration
(1 : 20).

What in fact will happen to him he does not know.
And it does not really matter, because this manifestation
of Christ can take place both through life and through
death. Elsewhere Paul speaks of his existence as carrying
round in his body the 'dying of Christ' (2 Cor 4 : 10).
Precisely at this point the language of the epistle becomes
irregular and broken. Both life and death offer such exciting possibilities that Paul's tongue stumbles as his
thought switches from one to the other. For him 'to live
is Christ'; death is only another way of being with Christ,
and one that Paul conceives as more intimate, hence a
'gain'. The apostle admits that he would choose death
were he absolutely free ('my desire', 1 : 23). This desire
is not negative. Nothing in the context suggests a repug-
nance for the burden of life. What sways Paul is exclusively the attraction of Christ. From the mode of being
that Paul now enjoys Christ has passed to another life
that the apostle wishes to share. It was as simple as that.

Here we must pause to note how Paul's theology
evolved under the pressure of circumstances. When he
wrote his first letter to the Thessalonians Paul fully expected that Christ would return within his lifetime. 'We

who are alive, who are left until the coming of the Lord, shall not precede those who have fallen asleep. For the Lord himself will descend from heaven with a cry of command, and with the archangel's call, and with the sound of the trumpet of God. And the dead in Christ shall arise first, then we who are alive, who are left, shall be caught up together with them in the cloud to meet the Lord in the air, and so we shall always be with the Lord' (1 Thess 4 : 15–17). The last phrase 'to be with the Lord' is parallel to 'to be with Christ' in Colossians. Paul's view of the goal of life has not changed, but an experience in Asia, perhaps the imprisonment mentioned in Philippians, which brought him close to death (cf 2 Cor 1 : 8–11) forced him to consider the possibility of his own death before the return of Christ. Would there be a long period of waiting until the final general resurrection of the body (cf Phil 3 : 21)? Had he remained within Jewish categories of thought Paul's answer would have to have been negative, because for the semites man was a unity. The Greeks, however, thought of man as a combination of body (material) and soul (spiritual), and the apostle's terminology here betrays the influence of this philosophy which Paul adopted because it permitted him to envisage a way of being with Christ without the body (cf also 2 Cor 5 : 1–10).

In this matter, however, Paul refuses to let his personal preference dominate his judgement, and he finally decides that 'to remain in the flesh is more necessary on your account' (1 : 24). His attitude here exemplifies what was said above (Phil 1 : 9) regarding the moral judgement of the christian. The apostle was faced with a choice between what was best for him personally and what was best for the community as a whole. To have chosen what was best for him personally would have been an egocentric decision that is the antithesis of being-in-Christ because it isolates the believer from his fellows. Life in Christ is a shared existence, and the one criterion of an authentic decision is: does it concretise and actualise that sharing? In choosing life Paul is thinking exclusively of others. The possibility of service has taken preeminence over personal satisfaction. And one needs the vision of love to see the multiform possibilities of service.

The service that Paul conceives himself as rendering to the Philippians concerns their 'progress and joy in the faith' (1 : 25). Faith, for the apostle, was without doubt a divine gift, but he can and does speak of himself and his collaborators as 'God's co-workers . . . through whom you believed' (1 Cor 3 : 9, 5). In the divine plan human instrumentality is involved in both the genesis and development of faith. Preaching obviously plays a role, both as proclamation and as exhortation, but it is significant that here Paul speaks of his 'presence'. His being among them is more significant than his words. 'what you have learned and received and heard and *seen* in me, do. And the God of peace will be with you' (Phil 4 : 9). The same idea is expressed more graphically elsewhere: 'Be imitators of me, as I am an imitator of Christ' (1 Cor 11 : 1). These texts are supremely important for the understanding of the role of authority in a faith-community. The authority figure must so incarnate the ideal of the community that he inspires the other members to continually deepen their commitment. The faith-community exists in response to a divine call expressed in the form of a person, Christ. In himself and in his relation with God he is what man is destined to be. But Christ is no longer with us. Hence the divine demand must be rearticulated in a personal form, that is, in a personality who can say with utter conviction 'for me to live is Christ' (Phil 1 : 21) and 'it is no longer I who live but Christ who lives in me' (Gal 2 : 20). Only with such a leader can there be progress and joy in the faith. If Paul's mere coming to the Philippians is a manifestation of the power of Christ, how much more his life among them.

1. How should a christian refute a charge based on the imputation of false motives?

2. Why cannot the christian make a moral decision on the basis of what is best for him alone?

3. Is an institutionalized authority structure compatible with Paul's understanding of the function of authority in the christian community?

4. How can institutional and personal authority be reconciled?

Phil 1:27–30. Exhortation to steadfastness

Paul devotes the rest of this letter to a series of appeals. In turn he emphasises the importance of steadfastness, unity through humility, and obedient selflessness if the Philippians are really to live in Christ.

In the first exhortation we get a glimpse into the situation at Philippi. Paul appeals to the members of the community not to let themselves be 'frightened' by their opponents. The implication is that the tactic employed by these latter is the threat or exercise of physical force. This interpretation is confirmed by the allusion to the suffering of the Philippians (1 : 29). It is extremely unlikely that these opponents are the judaizers who caused so much trouble in the other communities under the apostle's care, because in their case what Paul feared was that believers would be seduced away from the faith. There is no instance of their threatening the believers as a means to achieving their end. The suggestion that force was used makes it almost certain that the adversaries here were the pagan citizens of Philippi. This accords perfectly with what we know from other sources. Acts 16:21 reveals that the citizens thought of themselves as Romans, and this was justified because Anthony settled a number of his disbanded veterans there after his defeat of Brutus and Cassius (the assassins of Julius Caesar) at the battle of Philippi in 42 BC, and as a result gave the city the status of a 'colony', ie a military settlement with exceptional civic privileges. Roman influence was intensified twelve years later when Octavian, having defeated Anthony and Cleopatra, moved Latin-speaking settlers from Italy to Philippi in order to make room at home for his loyal veterans whom he hoped would constitute a dependable reserve for times of need. Given such a population the imperial cult must have flourished; inscriptions found in the ruins attest the worship of Julius, Augustus and Claudius. If, as seems likely, the christians of Philippi were Roman citizens, there would have been a strong social pressure on them to participate in the official cult of the city, because such participation was not a privilege but an obligation. It was part of the duties of a citizen.

This placed the Philippians in a very awkward position. They enjoyed the privileges of citizens but refused certain duties which could be onerous financially. Paul's advice is very practical. He tells them to stick together and present their irate fellow citizens with a united front. He does not advocate a complete break. He commands them to fulfil their duties as citizens, but in a manner

worthy of the gospel of Christ (1: 27a). They have to
reject those duties incompatible with their following of
Christ. Paul recognizes that this will bring suffering, but
contrary to what we might expect this is a cause for joy
not sorrow. They are fortunate that they have been given
the privilege of manifesting their faith in this way. Here
once again we see Paul's understanding of the value of
existential witness. Action, not words, is the criterion of
sincerity. Implicit in Paul's allusion to his own sufferings
at Philippi (1: 30; cf Acts 16: 22–24) is a reference to the
'partnership' mentioned in Phil 1: 5. The cooperation
begun then is now intensified by the fact that both he
and they are suffering in the same contest.

Paul's attitude towards this problem is identical with
that of Jesus: 'Render to Caesar the things that are
Caesar's, and to God the things that are God's' (Mk 12:
17). Worship is something due to the true God alone.
The fact that the Romans of Philippi thought otherwise
did not, however, blind Paul to the real values to be
found in the pagan environment of the christian community. Hence, at the end of this letter he exhorts the
believers: 'whatever is true, whatever is honourable,
whatever is just, whatever is pure, whatever is lovely,
whatever is gracious, if there is any excellence, if there
is anything worthy of praise, think about these things'
(4: 8). None of the terms in this list is specifically christian; all were current in pagan texts concerning the vir-
tuous life. The pagans did not always practice what they
preached (cf Rom 1: 18–32), but Paul here recognizes
that they had ideals which reflected the aspirations of our
nature. These he recommends without hesitation or
qualification to christians. He was fully aware of the
ravages of sin, but he was confident that the things which

were considered honourable by good men everywhere were in fact worthy of honour. If from one point of view christianity is an otherworldly religion, from another it is a humanism. One of the basic lessons of the incarnation is that followers of Christ must become *men*. God's gift and demand in Christ permits man to become what he was always intended to be. In formulating this ideal in concrete terms by means of his moral directives, Paul draws indiscriminately on the teaching of Jesus, the precepts of the OT, and the insights of pagan philosophers. No better proof could be given of the universality—and of the validity—of man's basic aspirations. For Paul these are worthy of the christian's most profound attention, but their integration into existence in Christ must be controlled by the insight and sensitivity born of genuine love (cf Phil 1 : 9).

1. What should be the christian's attitude towards his environment?

2. What, if any, is the value of the distinction between 'sacred' and 'profane'? Can you think of a human value that is exclusively 'sacred' or 'profane'?

3. Does today's state worship any 'false gods'? If so, what criterion is used to detect them?

3

The great hymn
Phil 2:1–11

Phil 2 : 1–5. Exhortation to unity through selflessness

Dogmatically this is the most important section of the
epistle, because in order to support his appeal for complete harmony Paul proposes the example of the attitude
of Christ as expressed in a primitive christian hymn. A
similar exhortation is to be found in Rom 15 : 1–5, but
there the quotation of the hymn is replaced by a citation
from the OT.

The exhortation really begins in 2 : 2. 2 : 1 represents
an effort to dispose the Philippians to see the necessity
of what is being asked of them. It is beautifully paraphrased by Lightfoot. 'If then your experience in Christ
appeals to you with any force, if love exerts any persuasive power upon you, if your fellowship in the Spirit is
a living reality, if you have any affectionate yearnings of
heart, any tender feelings of compassion, listen and obey'.
The apostle is talking to men who for some time now
have lived 'in Christ', that is, as members of the whole
Christ, and he endeavours to integrate his appeal into
their lives by appealing to their deepest experiences as
christians and their most noble impulses as men. He is
convinced that in their initial efforts to live their commitment to Christ they must have perceived, however
vaguely, the values of fellowship, love, and compassion.

What he now asks them is to manifest these values con-
cretely in their pattern of living.

For Paul the mode of being proper to man without
Christ was characterised by isolation. The individual becomes the centre of his own private world. Not only does
he selfishly withdraw from others, but he acts in such a
way as to repulse others: 'Full of envy, murder, strife,
deceit, malignity, they are gossips, slanderers, haters of
God, insolent, haughty, boastful, inventors of evil, dis-
obedient to parents, foolish, faithless, heartless, ruthless'
(Rom 1 : 29–31; cf similar lists in Gal 5 : 19–21; 1 Cor
6 : 9–10; 2 Cor 12 : 20; Col 3 : 5–9). Man in Christ, on the
contrary, is one who shares with others. It is debatable
whether Paul could have conceived of an anonymous
christian, but it is certain that for him the idea of an
autonomous christian would have been a contradiction
in terms. In baptism the believer has 'put on Christ',
which is at the same time a putting on of 'the new man'.
This terminology presumes that a radical transformation
has taken place which gives the individual an entirely
new orientation, but if we look at the context in which
Paul uses these terms it immediately becomes obvious
that this individualistic interpretation does not exhaust
his meaning. 'As many of you as were baptized into Christ
have put on Christ. There is neither Jew nor Greek, there
is neither slave or freeman, there is neither male or
female, for *you are all one in Christ Jesus*' (Gal 3 : 27–28).
'You have put on the new man . . . *where* there cannot be
Greek and Jew, circumcised and uncircumcised, bar-
barian, Scythian, slave, freeman, but Christ is all in all'
(Col 3 : 10). Without in any way diminishing the individ-
uality of the believers, being-in-Christ is a corporate,
shared existence which is concretised and realised by

'loving'. The virtues of the 'new man' are all other-directed: 'Put on then . . . compassion, kindness, lowliness, meekness, and patience, forbearing one another, and if one has a complaint against another forgiving each other; as the Lord has forgiven you so must you also forgive. And above all these put on love which binds everything together in perfect harmony' (Col 3 : 12–14; cf Gal 5 : 22–23; Rom 12 : 1–21).

Being a realist, Paul recognised that there would always be a gap between this ideal and the actual pattern of living of the christian community. There would always be room for intensive growth (cf Eph 4 : 11–16). Hence his frequent exhortations which have a twofold purpose. His negative directives are designed to alert the believer to the danger of slipping back into the state of isolation proper to man without Christ, eg 'Do nothing out of selfishness or conceit' (Phil 2 : 3), ie never act for motives of selfish ambition, for this only serves to create factions within the community, or for the sake of personal vanity. His positive precepts are calculated to bring the ideal of complete sharing closer to realization, eg 'Look not to your own interests, but rather to those of others' (Phil 2 : 4).

If these directives are followed, the Philippians will share a unified attitude ('mind') towards life which will manifest itself in love, in complete harmony of feelings and affections, and in the direction of their thoughts to a single end (Phil 2 : 2). 'Mind' in the broad sense of attitude or disposition also appears in 2 : 5, which links the exhortation with the hymn which follows. Translated literally this verse reads, 'Have this attitude in you *which also in* Christ Jesus'. The lack of a verb in the second part of the sentence makes the interpretation difficult. What is to be supplied? To a great extent the answer depends on the sense given to 'in Christ Jesus'. If this phrase is understood as a reference to the historical Jesus then we must supply 'was': 'Have this mind among yourselves which was in Christ Jesus' (RSV). In this interpretation Paul exhorts the Philippians to the imitation of Christ; his life is the model for christian living. As he 'humbled himself' (1:8) so must the believers 'in humility count others better than yourselves' (2:3). However, in 2:1 'in Christ' means the whole Christ, the christian community united with its head. If 'in Christ Jesus' is understood in the same way we must supply the verb 'to have': 'Have this attitude among yourself which also you ought to have in Christ Jesus'. In this interpretation it is a question of the attitude appropriate to those whose existence is 'in Christ', and the link with 2:1 reveals how perfectly this meaning harmonises with the context.

It is extremely difficult to choose between these two interpretations, but perhaps a choice is not necessary. One does not necessarily exclude the other. In fact they are complementary. The christian community is a reincarnation of Christ. For the whole and for each of its members the mission of Christ was the one event that really mattered. Both individually and collectively the believers must mirror his attitude.

Phil 2:6–11. The christological hymn

The development on the attitude of Christ is couched in a rhythmic language which has led all commentators to infer the presence of a hymn quoted by the apostle. A similar hymn is cited in Col 1:15–20. Even in the last century the Philippian hymn had given rise to such a variety of interpretations that an author writing in 1876 said that their diversity was 'enough to fill the student with despair and to afflict him with intellectual paralysis'. That sombre appraisal is even more justified today. While no consensus on the overall meaning of the hymn has emerged, it is generally recognized that one must begin with an analysis of its structure.

The classic analysis of Lohmeyer is reproduced in the JB translation, although the layout does not reveal clearly enough that his arrangement involved six stanzas each of three lines. This solution, however, does not stand up to detailed analysis, because it fails to take into account the inner parallelisms of the hymn. If these are given their due value we arrive at the following structure.

I

1 Who, being in the form of God
2 did not consider it a prize to be equal to God
3 but he emptied himself
4 taking the form of a slave.

II

1 Having become in the likeness of men
2 and being found in shape as a man
3 he humbled himself
4 becoming obedient unto death.

III

1 Therefore, God super-exalted him
2 and gave him the Name which is above all names
3 so that at the name of Jesus every knee should bow
4 and every voice proclaim: 'The Lord is Jesus Christ'.

Stanzas I and II are identical in structure. Each begins with a participle linked to the preposition 'in'. In the second line the thought of the first is continued by means of a comparative term (I, 2 'equal'; II, 2 'as'). The third line contains the principal verb (I, 3 'he emptied'; II, 3 'he humbled') whose object is in each case the reflexive pronoun 'himself'. The fourth line develops the meaning of the key verb by means of a participle (I, 4 'taking'; II, 4 'becoming'). Note also that one term from the first line is repeated in the second (I, 1 and 2 'God'; II, 1 and 2 'man'), and that another term from the first line is reproduced in the fourth (I, 1 and 4 'form'; II, 1 'having become', 4 'becoming').

The conclusion to be drawn from this detailed structural similarity is that stanzas I and II are to be considered together. This is reinforced by the 'Therefore' which begins stanza III and obviously marks a major turning point in the thought of the hymn. In this stanza lines 1 and 2 exhibit the stylistic feature known as synonymous parallelism, ie the thought of both lines is identical but the words are different. A similar parallelism is to be found in lines 3 and 4. The unity of the stanza is assured by the correspondence between the two parts because the bowing of the knee (line 3) is related to the exaltation of Jesus (line 1), and the proclamation (line 4) is a reference to the name (line 2).

If the version of the hymn given above is compared with that in the RSV or JB it will be seen that three phrases have been omitted: 'death on a cross' immediately after II, 4; 'in heaven, on earth, and under the earth' immediately after III, 3; and 'to the glory of God the Father' immediately after III, 4. Since these obscure and even distort the careful structure discerned above they must be considered later additions to the original hymn. This conclusion is confirmed by the observation that all three phrases are found at the end of lines, and that the additions to III, 3 and III, 4 are rather awkwardly separated from the terms by which they are governed. 'In heaven, on earth, and under the earth' is governed by 'knee', and 'to the glory of God the Father' by 'proclaim'. Similar additions have been made to the christological hymn in Col 1 : 15–20.

Where did this hymn come from? Some terms in the hymn reflect ideas found in other pauline letters. For example, the apostle presents Christ to the Corinthians as 'the man from heaven' (1 Cor 15 : 47), who 'being rich, impoverished himself for your sakes' (2 Cor 8 : 9). On the other hand, the hymn also contains words and theological ideas that are found nowhere else in the pauline letters. For example, Paul never speaks of Jesus as being 'equal' with God, and the idea that God rewarded Christ for his 'obedience' with 'the name' is foreign to his thought. These indications which point in different directions can be reconciled by the hypothesis that the author was not Paul but a christian belonging to one of the communities he had founded who rethought pauline ideas in a highly personal way. This hypothesis is confirmed by the pauline character of the additions. It is unlikely that the apostle would feel the need to retouch a hymn that he had written himself. How the hymn was originally used is still unclear. There is not enough evidence to permit a choice between a baptismal and a eucharistic liturgical celebration.

Stanzas I and II

One fundamental question underlies all discussions about the meaning of this hymn: does the initial 'Who' (I, 1) refer to the historical incarnate Jesus, or to the word prior to the incarnation? If one says that it is a reference to the word then stanza 1 is concerned with the renunciation implicit in the incarnation, and stanza II deals with the further renunciation of the passion. On the other hand, if one maintains that 'Who' refers to the historical Jesus, there is no reference to the incarnation and the chief preoccupation of both stanzas is the passion.

The importance of the question is obvious. The answer given it will necessarily condition the interpretation of the details of the text. Hence we must begin with the key verbs. Our original question can be rephrased in this form: is 'he emptied himself' (I, 3) identical in meaning with 'he humbled himself' (II, 3)? If the answer is affirmative, both stanzas must have the passion in mind.

There is no doubt about the meaning of 'he humbled himself' (II, 3), because the following phrase 'becoming obedient unto death' (II, 4) can only refer to the passion, as the pauline addition 'death on a cross' makes doubly clear. Hence we must concentrate our attention on 'he emptied himself' (I, 3) which is qualified by 'taking the form of a slave' (I, 4). This latter phrase is so cryptic that it affords no clue to the interpretation of the main statement. Only when the sense of 'he emptied himself' has been determined will the meaning of 'taking the form of a slave' become clear.

In the Greek OT the verb translated by 'he emptied' is used both in a literal and in a metaphorical sense. The former is illustrated by Gen 24:20 ('She quickly emptied her jar into the trough and ran again to the well to draw'), and the latter by Jer 15:9 ('She who bore seven has languished; she has swooned away'). In the latter text the strength of the distressed mother has ebbed away and she is reduced to weakness. The same imagery underlies 'We must needs die, and are as water spilt upon the ground' (2 Sam 14:14). By introducing the idea of death this passage directs our attention to a text in one of the servant songs, where, speaking of the mysterious servant of Yahweh, it is said that 'he poured out his soul unto death' (Is 53:12). We have here an exact parallel to 'he emptied himself', because semitic writers used 'soul' in the sense of 'self'; eg 'Behold my servant whom I have chosen, my beloved with whom my soul is (= I am) well pleased' (Is 42:1—a good example of synonymous parallelism).

Once this close contact with the Isaian text has been noted, the conclusion that 'he emptied himself' is an allusion to the *death* of Jesus becomes inescapable. The validity of interpreting this statement in the light of the servant song is confirmed by the light that this prophecy throws on other details of the hymn. The humiliation (cf II, 3) of the servant is the theme of Is 53:1–9, and this suffering was willed by God; 'It was the will of the Lord to bruise him; he has put him to grief' (Is 53:10). This explains the 'obedience' (II, 4) of Jesus, which, incidentally, was 'unto death'—the precise words of Is 53:12. Here we must pause to underline one important point of difference between the hymn and the servant song. The Isaian text strongly underlines the obedience and submission of the servant (cf Is 53:7), and this aspect, as we have seen, is reflected in the hymn. The hymn, however, goes further because Jesus is the subject of the verbs 'he emptied himself' and 'he humbled himself'. Thus the hymn stresses the voluntary character of the passion. Death was not imposed on him. He chose it freely out of love.

At this stage the meaning of 'taking the form of a slave' (I, 4) becomes clear. The Greek term translated by 'slave' is used in Is 49:3, 5 (another servant song) to translate 'servant'. This passage also throws light on the hymn. 'You are my servant (= slave) in whom I will be glorified. But I (= the servant) said: I have laboured in vain. I have spent my strength for nothing and vanity. Yet surely my right is with the Lord, and my recompense with my God' (Is 49:3–4). Here again we have the idea of strength being poured out under obedience to God. The effort is futile in terms of tangible results, but it is God who rewards. It is the structure 'obedient service—reward' that links stanzas I–II with stanza III. In this perspective the word 'form' in the expression 'taking the form of a slave' (I, 4) would appear to mean 'a form or mode of existence', namely, that appropriate to the servant. Scholars agree that 'form' is not a synonym for 'substance'; the metaphysical concern of later dogmatic theology is not that of the author of the hymn. His interest is in the saving character of Jesus' life and mission, which he bring out by means of allusions to the mission of the servant who made vicarious satisfaction for the sins of his people.

It has now become evident that I, 3–4 and II, 3–4 are in synonymous parallelism, ie though the words are different, 'he emptied himself taking the form of a slave' is identical in meaning with 'he humbled himself becoming obedient unto death'. Now we are in a position to say

that the identity of structure noted above is confirmed
by identity of meaning. This conclusion gives us a clue
to the meaning of I, 1-2 ('Who, being in the form of God
did not consider it a prize to be equal to God') and II, 1-2
('Having become in the likeness of men and being found
in appearance as a man'). The identity of structure and
the synonymous parallelism of I, 3-4 and II, 3-4 suggests
that they also stand in parallelism. In their case, however, the parallelism must be antithetic, ie what is fundamentally the same idea is looked at from radically opposed viewpoints; eg 'a wise son gives joy to his father;
a stupid child angers his mother' (Prov 10:1—this chapter contains a multitude of other examples).

The antithesis here is between divine (I, 1-2 : God) and
human (II, 1-2 : man). Note the similarity in construction
of the first lines: 'in the form of God' (I, 1), 'in the likeness of men' (II, 1). Both are predicated of the historical
Jesus. Here we find the historical beginning of a line of
theological speculation that eventually culminated in the
definition that Jesus enjoyed two 'natures', one divine,
the other human. These categories, however, were not
present in the mind of the author of this hymn. He is
thinking of modes of existence, not as manifesting different natures, but manifested by different types of activity.
In other words, his categories are dynamic rather than
static.

To illustrate this we have to turn once again to the
OT. Adam was made 'in the image of God' (Gen 1:26;
'in the likeness of God', 5:1, 3), and through Eve the
serpent tempted him 'to be like God' (Gen 3:5). In both
these texts it is a question of activities exercised by man,
in one case the exercise of dominion over the animals,
and in the other moral knowledge. The purpose of this

allusion to the creation narrative was simply to show the
way in which the terminology of the hymn could be used.
However, it also gives us a second clue to the understanding of the phrase 'in the form of God', because the
Hebrew term that is translated as 'image' in Gen 1:26
is translated by 'form' elsewhere in the Greek OT. Hence
'form' and 'image' may be used interchangably, and 1, 1
may be paraphrased, 'Who, being in the image of God';
cf 'Who is the image of the invisible God' (Col 1:15).
Again, in the Greek OT the idea of 'glory' was intimately
associated with the notions of 'form' and 'image'. As
applied to God in the OT 'glory' connotes a manifestation
of God characterised by radiant splendour and rendered
accessible to human experience by the accompanying
action. Thus Paul terms Christ 'the Lord of glory' while
thinking of the power of his deeds. It is very probable
that the author of the hymn was thinking along the same
lines, because in the light of the resurrection the eye of
faith could see in the earthly ministry of Jesus a manifestation of divine power. This relationship of Jesus to
the Father in terms of power was the antecedent of the
understanding of this relationship in terms of being. The
first probable reference to Jesus as 'God' is found in Rom
9:5, and all the certain instances of 'God' used as a title
for Jesus are much later than this letter. To sum up:
'being in the form of God' means that Jesus disposed of
the power of God. This obviously supposes that there was
a special relationship between Jesus and God, but this is
not the immediate concern of the author of the hymn.

His thought focuses on what Jesus did with this power
(1, 2). and the point he makes is that Jesus did not use
it selfishly. He did not regard it as 'a piece of good luck',
or 'a lucky find' to be gloated over. The same under-

standing of the ministry of Jesus may be illustrated by
two passages from the gospels. The first is the temptation
narrative where Jesus refused the selfish use of his power
(Mt 4: 1–11; Lk 4: 1–13), and the second appears in
Matthew's version of the arrest of Jesus. Jesus is presented
as saying, 'Do you think that I cannot appeal to my
Father, and he will at once send me more than twelve
legions of angels? But how then would the scriptures be
fulfilled, that it must be so?' (Mt 26: 53–54). From their
experience of the power of the risen Christ some of the
first christian theologians inferred that this power must
also have been enjoyed by the historical Jesus who was
the same person. To have used this power to save himself
from his passion would have been to act counter to the
will of his Father who had decreed that his mission was
to be accomplished in humiliation and suffering. The
rabbis spoke of a son who rejected paternal authority as
one who makes himself equal with his father (cf Jn 5: 18).
To have acted independently of God would have been
to destroy Jesus' quality as the image or form of God.

Precisely the same idea is expressed in very different
words in II, 1–2. 'Being in the likeness of men and being
found in appearance as a man' means simply that Jesus
lived, acted, and died as men do. He could have done
otherwise but he chose not to out of obedience to the
will of his Father. Nonetheless there is a certain hesitation and caution perceptible in the terminology used
which demands an explanation. Why is there no clear,
unambiguous statement that Jesus was man? It is not
that the author of the hymn had any doubt about the
fact. His hesitation sprang from the realization that there
was something more than human in him. Just at this
point in the development of theological reflection on the

mystery of the person of Jesus it had come to be recognized that 'man', while accurate in the strictest sense, was not a completely satisfactory category to describe Jesus. Thus the author of the hymn shrank from too close an identification. The best he could do to express his understanding of the mystery was to confront his readers with the phrases 'in the form of God' and 'in the likeness of men'. By the strict identity of his hymnic formulation he tried to ensure that one would not be emphasised at the expense of the other.

Stanza III

The beginning of this verse clearly marks a decisive turning-point in the hymn. Not only does the initial 'therefore' claim our attention, but it directs it to a shift of emphasis. In stanzas I and II the principal actor was Jesus. In stanza III it is God. He now takes the initiative in vindicating the Jesus who emptied and humbled himself through obedience. What God has done for Jesus is expressed in synonymous parallelism 'he super-exalted him and gave him the name which is above all names' (III, 1–2). Here once again we have a contact with an Isaian servant song. 'Behold my servant shall understand, and shall be super-exalted, and shall be extolled most highly' (Is 52 : 13). The greatness of the reward is commensurate with the depth of humiliation accepted by Jesus.

The name above all names is that which in the OT was the exclusive property of God, and which distinguished the God of Israel from all rivals and idol powers, namely, 'Lord'. This is made explicit by the confessional proclamation 'The Lord is Jesus Christ' (III, 4). The fundamental meaning of 'Lord' is rulership based on power. It is, therefore, essentially a functional term. In III, 3 it is specifically underlined that this is now the name of Jesus. It is not improbable that the author of the hymn had in mind the etymological value of this name, 'He who saves', for this is certainly the function that Jesus exercises as Lord. Those who proclaim him Lord are those who have felt his power in their lives; 'no one can say "Jesus is Lord" except by the Holy Spirit' (1 Cor 12:3). They naturally hope that one day every voice and every knee (cf Is 45:23) will recognise the universal sovereignty of Jesus the saviour.

1. Writing in today's idiom how would you express the insight into the mystery of the person of Jesus contained in this hymn?

2. What ideas would you have particular difficulty with, and why?

3. Has later christological speculation been faithful to the insight of this hymn?

4

Letter B continued
Phil 2:12–3:1; 4:2–9

Phil 2:12–18. Exhortation to witness

The link between this exhortation and the preceding is
the theme of obedience. The saving death of Jesus is the
self-giving that founded the christian community whose
members are to exhibit a similar selflessness in their dealings with others (2:1–4). The obedience that is in
question here is not an automatic acceptance of the
apostle's directives. Paul never speaks directly about
obedience to the law, to commandments, or even to God's
will. Following immediately on the proclamation that
concludes the hymn, this obedience can only be the complete acceptance of Jesus as Lord. It is in the reduction
of this submission to a pattern of practical living that
the believer works out his salvation. While Paul was with
them the Philippians had the stimulus of his presence,
but despite his absence they are not alone. In responding
to the love of God manifested and offered to them in the
person of Christ they have satisfied the conditions for
God's personal presence (as distinct from his causal presence as creator) among them. Since love delights in activity for the beloved, they are assured of God's energising
influence in their lives.

By corresponding to the persuasive influence of love
they will not only benefit themselves, but their lives will

influence others. 2 : 14–16 is the key to the understanding of Paul's theology of witness. 'World' here is not the physical universe, but the sphere constituted by the complex of human relationships. In this context it has a pejorative connotation, because it is the sphere constituted by a degenerate generation consumed by egoism and jealousy. Paul's pessimistic view is rooted in the social conditions of the port cities of the eastern Mediterranean in which he exercised his ministry, but it is also coloured by his awareness of the new possibilities of existence revealed to humanity by Christ. Men to whom these have not been made known cannot realize their full potentialities. They are dragged down to something less than human by the essentially self-centred cultural context in which they are immersed. Elsewhere Paul speaks of this state as an enslavement by sin. He conceives the cumulative force of past and present personal sins as a force so potent that in order to bring out its impact it must be personalized.

It is in this situation that the christians 'hold forth the word of life.' This is another facet of the Philippians' 'partnership in the gospel' (1 : 5), and the significant point to note is that they play their role not by saying something but by doing something. It is not a question of verbal proclamation of the gospel. Paul's stress on the virtues of the Philippians makes it clear that their preaching consists in the quality of their lives. Inevitably, then, their message is a 'word of life' (a term the apostle never employs for the preached gospel). Their being what they are demonstrates the possibility of a new dimension of existence which is radically different from what man has been accustomed to expect of himself. Left to his own resources man is overwhelmed by a sense of his own weakness. Torn by the contradictions of his nature (cf Rom 7) he despairs of finding within himself the fulfilment that he knows from bitter experience is not to be found in matter. To him the radiant bearing of the believers is a message of hope. It witnesses to the fact that they are no longer enmeshed in the limitations suffocating him, that they have found a source of life and strength whose need he now experiences more keenly than ever before. This provocation of dissatisfaction with the *status quo* is of the essence of witness. In those who through union with Christ have realised the possibilities open to humanity man is confronted with the promise of salvation in a way that he cannot ignore.

Paul sees this apostolic orientation of the christian life as the prolongation of his own mission. This, coupled with the fact that from another point of view it is simply the working out of their salvation, is a cause for rejoicing, both for him and for the Philippians. The cultic terminology of 2 : 17 graphically underlines the union between the two partners. The life of the community, which is nothing but the concrete expression of their faith, is a sacrifice (cf Rom 12 : 1) to which Paul may be related as the 'drink-offering' or libation. He is not sure how his imprisonment is going to turn out. It has meant humiliation and suffering. It may mean death. Nonetheless, his life and theirs constitute a unique act of worship, the new sacrifice of the new Lord. It is the total giving of self, not a symbolic giving through material gifts.

1. In speaking of the death of God is the reference to his personal presence or his causal presence?

2. Is it accurate to say that God's invitation to personal presence is primarily mediated by the witness value of the life of a christian community?

3. *What conclusions are to be drawn from Paul's concept of witness regarding the role of the layman in the church?*

Phil 2:19–30. Announcement of plans

It is obvious that when Paul wrote these words he had no intention of writing the long warning that constitutes Phil 3 in the present form of this epistle. He is bringing letter B to an end with news about his collaborators particularly well known to the Philippians; compare the ending of Colossians (4:7–18).

It is reasonable to assume that Epaphroditus is to be the bearer of this letter (B). He was the delegate of the Philippian community who brought their gift to Paul. It is this gift that is in question in letter A. While with Paul he fell ill, and the news got back to his friends at Philippi. Not only that, but Epaphroditus, who is still with Paul, knows how much concern this has caused them. It would be incredible if Paul had not used one of these contacts to thank the Philippians for their gift. In all likelihood letter A went back with those who brought the news of Epaphroditus' illness to Philippi.

It is a little curious that Paul should feel it necessary to warn the Philippians to receive Epaphroditus 'with all joy' and honour (2:29), but perhaps the apostle was afraid that he was in danger of being accused of leaving Paul at a time when his services might be needed. Paul's motive in sending Epaphroditus back to Philippi was not simply the feeling that his recovery might be speeded by the atmosphere of his home community. He does so 'that

I might be less sorrowful' (2:28). One has the impression that there is something wrong at Philippi, and that Paul hopes that Epaphroditus will be able to set it right. This inference is confirmed by the unique build-up that he is given: 'my brother and fellow-worker and companion-in-arms . . . honour such men for he nearly died for the work of Christ, risking his life to complete your service to me' (2:25, 29–30). This can be understood as the expression of a desire to strengthen the authority of Epaphroditus.

Paul knew that the Philippians would be concerned about the outcome of his imprisonment and so he promises that as soon as it is known he will send Timothy with the news (2:23). Timothy was with Paul when he first brought the gospel to Philippi (Acts 16), and what Paul says of him reveals their deep friendship. The translation 'I have no one like him' (2:20) does not at all render the force of the Greek. The apostle uses the adjective 'equal-souled' to describe one who shares his aspirations so profoundly as to be another self. Note that the one virtue explicitly mentioned is selflessness (2:21). As Paul himself (cf 1 Cor 11:1), Timothy mirrors the christian ideal (cf Phil 2:1–11).

Phil 3:1. Conclusion and postscript (4:2–9)

The initial 'Finally' clearly indicates the conclusion of the letter. What appears in the RSV as 'rejoice in the Lord' can be translated with equal accuracy as 'Farewell in the Lord'. The two ideas are not mutually exclusive, and the paraphrase of the *New English Bible* brings out what was probably Paul's meaning: 'and now, friends, farewell: I wish you joy in the Lord'.

The second part of 3:1 causes difficulty, because though Paul announces that he is going to repeat himself ('to write the same things' = 'to repeat the same pleas'), nothing in ch 3 can be considered to belong to this category. This chapter concerns an entirely new problem to which no allusion has been made in either of the two letters considered so far. This is one of the main reasons for considering 3:2–4:1 to have been an originally independent letter. It is only in the section 4:2–9 that we begin to encounter themes that have appeared in letter B.

In 4:2 we have a specific application of the pleas for unity in 1:27 and 2:1–4. Two women of the community are in disagreement, and Paul appeals to them by name to solve their differences. It is not impossible that the apostle had this case in mind when he wrote 'do nothing from party spirit or vain ambition' (2:3). If so, each would have felt that her talents and services entitled her to a superior place, At first Paul did not intend to say anything about this affair in the letter addressed to the whole community. We know that sometimes he preferred to handle certain delicate matters orally, eg 'About the other things I will give directions when I come' (1 Cor 11:34). The build-up given Epaphroditus, and the lessening in Paul's anxiety that his presence would bring (4:25, 28) suggests that the apostle's original intention was to give him an oral message for these two ladies. At the last moment, however, he felt that this might not be sufficient. The situation was highly explosive, and unless clamped down quickly and decisively, an outburst might divide the community. Hence the postscript, which is in effect a public reprimand expressed with scrupulous impartiality.

Note, however, that Paul says that these women 'have laboured side by side with me in the gospel together with Clement and the rest of my fellow workers' (4:3). There is no hint of any discrimination against a so-called weaker sex. From the account of the coming of the gospel to Philippi in Acts it seems that the first converts were all women (Acts 16:13–15). Unfortunately we have no information as to what role Euodia and Syntyche played in the subsequent life of the community. That they were strong and dominant personalities seems implied in Paul's fear that their quarrel would divide the community. One wonders if the injunction of 1 Cor 14:34 was observed at Philippi!

It is tempting to translate 3:4 'I bid you farewell in the Lord, always. Again, I say, Farewell', but the 'always' makes it a little artificial. The traditional rendering (RSV) is perfectly in place, because joy and kindliness (3:5—not 'forbearance or 'tolerance') should be the characteristics of the christian community. A joyous serenity in the face of the complexities and trials of life, and a consistent thoughtfulness for others manifest a quality of life that cannot fail to impress those who are searching for a meaningful existence, for peace in society and within themselves.

With another 'Finally, brethren' (4:8; cf 3:1), Paul again indicates that he is approaching the end of his letter. This time it is really the end, because as we saw 4:10–20 belongs to letter A. Paul concludes with an exhortation (4:8) which serves to balance somewhat his characterisation of the pagans of Philippi as a 'crooked and perverse generation' (2:15). They do have ethical ideals which the apostle recommends warmly to the christian community. Believers must be firmly integrated into the society in which they live if they are to influence it. Paul expressed this facet of his theology of witness very succinctly when writing to the Galatians: 'Brethren, I beseech you, become as I am, for I also have become as you are' (Gal 4: 12). By accepting the high ethical ideals of their environment the christians ensure themselves a degree of respect and understanding. But the life of the community comes to have witness value when these standards are put into practice by the majority and infused with joy, love and peace.

1. Does unity in the christian community depend on uniformity?

2. Paul stresses joy as a characteristic of the christian life. He also makes it very clear that suffering is indissolubly associated with a sincere effort to respond to the call of God in Christ. How can these be reconciled? What is christian joy?

5

Letter C
Phil 3:2–4:1

The tone of this letter is strikingly different from that of the other two. The depth of Paul's anxiety is manifested both by the virulence of his attack on those who are disturbing the community and by the emotional appeal to his own personal experience. There is no indication in the text itself that this letter was addressed to the Philippians, but it is difficult to see why it should have been combined with letters A and B had it not been addressed to the same community.

It is difficult to say whether the danger that so preoccupied Paul was a reality or only a possibility, but the latter seems more probable. While in Ephesus Paul had grave difficulties with the christian communities in Galatia and Corinth, who were disturbed by preachers controverting what had been taught by the apostle. These are generically termed 'judaisers' because they advocated the importance of Jewish religious observances either as a substitute for, or a complement to, the gospel. Since Philippi was bracketed by these two trouble-spots Paul had good reason to fear that the rot might spread there.

There is tremendous urgency in the thrice repeated 'Look out' (3 : 2), and savage sarcasm in the terms applied to the false teachers. He calls them 'dogs', thus turning

against Jews the scornful term that they employed for
gentiles (cf Mt 15:26), and contemptuously dismisses
circumcision as a 'mutilation'. Circumcision, of course,
was the key issue in the sense that it crystallised the opposition between the preaching of Paul and that of the
judaisers. For the latter salvation was essentially a matter
of belonging to the chosen people, and this belonging was
symbolised by circumcision. For Paul, on the other hand,
the fundamental element in salvation was a decision com-
mitting oneself totally to Christ. It is in this perspective
that we must understand the apostle's refusal to give
any importance to physical circumcision. It was an oper-
ation entirely external to the individual, and which did
not change him as a person in any way. Yet Paul can also
claim that 'we are the circumcision'; cf 'In him (Christ)
you were circumcised with a circumcision made without
hands by putting off the body of flesh' (Col 2:11).

The key to this paradox is the idea of 'flesh'. Circumcision was an actual cutting off of a particle of flesh. The
christian decision of faith was a putting off of the flesh.
Obviously 'flesh' is not used in the same way in both
these sentences. In the first it means a physical substance,
and in the second it means a mode of being. Used in this
second sense 'flesh' is contrasted with 'spirit'. These terms
are Paul's short-hand for designating respectively man's
mode of being without Christ, and man's mode of being
in Christ. The essential quality of life in the 'flesh' is
isolation. The types of activity that Paul finds most frequently associated with this state are such as to make a
true relationship with others impossible (cf Rom 1:29–
32; Gal 5:19–21; Col 3:5–9). The only way to make
such isolation bearable is for man to emphasise his independence and powers of achievement. Hence for Paul

one of the chief manifestations of life in the flesh is 'boasting', ie pride in one's personal achievement. This is what he means here when he speaks of 'putting one's confidence in the flesh' (Phil 3:3–4). This confidence is the supposed security that man builds up from the visible and tangible elements of his existence that he can control and deal with. Such a view, however, embodies a fundamental error. To imagine that the visible and the tangible constitute the whole of reality is to totally misconstrue the human situation. It is to forget the fact implied by the question, 'What do you have that you have not been given? And if it has been given you, why do you boast as if it had not been given you' (1 Cor 4:7).

This self-reliance is the antithesis of life in the 'spirit'. This is a mode of being in which man does not judge himself or understand himself in terms of the visible and tangible. He sees himself, first of all, as a creature dependent on and blessed by his creator. In appreciating the love shown by God in Christ he enters into a new relationship with God by recognising him as Father. In this perspective other men are seen, not as threats to his independence, but as brothers. Hence life in the 'spirit' is characterised, not by isolation, but by sharing. All exist in one body, the body of Christ.

Contrasting these two modes of existence Paul recognizes that whatever his personal accomplishments were (3:5–6), they are as nothing compared to what he has gained in Christ. Yet it is on precisely this sort of accomplishment that the judaisers lay such emphasis. If the Philippians really appreciated what they have they would be in no danger of seduction by the promises held out to them.

Hence Paul explicitly mentions the 'gains' of christianity. The very word-order of 3:10 parallels the events of his conversion as presented in Acts 9:3–16, but the 'I' of this passage is the 'I' of every christian. The culminating point of his list is, of course, the final resurrection. As we have seen, hope for final union with Christ is a theme that runs right through letter B (1:6, 10–11, 23; 4:5). It is a sharing with another, not an isolating personal achievement. This shared life which will one day flower into perfect union was inaugurated in baptism which is a dying and rising with Christ (cf Rom 6:1–11). Hence the first 'gain' of conversion is 'to know Christ in the power of his resurrection'.

But there is also another 'gain', namely, 'to know the fellowship of his sufferings'. Again the idea of sharing is stressed. The rather curious use of the word 'fellowship' introduces into this phrase the spirit of letter B. Union with the Christ who emptied and humbled himself (Phil 2:7–8) necessarily involves suffering. The inevitable tension between 'flesh' and 'spirit' (cf Rom 7:15–24) is an adequate explanation of why this must be so. The struggle to permit the impulse of the spirit to dominate is elsewhere spoken of as a continual act of dying, 'Wherever we go we carry always in our body the dying of Jesus, that the life of Jesus may be manifested in our body' (2 Cor 4:10). This citation provides us with the clue to the understanding of 'fellowship' here. In letter B Paul uses this term, or its synonyms, to express the close bond that unites the apostle and the community at Philippi in their common striving for the spread of the gospel. Both partners have suffered (1:17, 28). It is this sharing to which he now alludes. His own 'dying' is but a contribution to the suffering of the whole Christ which all christians must bear in order to bring the body of

Christ to full measure (cf Col 1:24; Eph 4:11–16). To one who has experienced true isolation and loneliness any 'fellowship', no matter how painful, is a privilege. How much more so, then, when this pain can be transmuted into a source of joy and peace for others (cf what was said above, apropos of Phil 2:14–16, regarding the witness value of a life in which 'spirit' triumphs over 'flesh').

Membership in the christian community is a privilege but it is not the seal on a perfection already achieved. Paul uses the terminology of the pagan mystery cults (3:12), but given the context it is difficult not to see an implicit contrast with judaism where simple belonging was the one thing that really counted. Paul's emphasis on his own struggle to attain a prize that lies in the future is intended to console and forewarn the Philippians, but at the same time it reveals that the church is not a community of the perfect. It is a setting which permits man to deepen his response to 'the call of God in Christ Jesus' (3:14). By immersing himself in an atmosphere of sincere mutual love the sensitivity of the believer to the practical applications of this call becomes progressively more refined (cf Phil 1:9). In obeying the voice of God thus expressed in the details of his life, the transformation initiated in baptism gradually affects more and more of his personality, so that 'we all . . . are being changed from glory to glory' (2 Cor 3:18). As Christ is the glory of God, ie his visible, effective manifestation, so believers become the glory of Christ as his image in them becomes progressively more manifest. The life of loving service demanded of the christian is designed to facilitate this transformation (cf Phil 2:1–11).

Paul seems to have some doubt that those at Philippi will all share this understanding of the church (3:15).

He plays on the idea of perfection by saying that those who are 'perfect' ('mature' RSV) will see that perfection for the christian is an on-going affair. He will never reach the stage where he can sit back and say, 'This is it'. But what about those who hold a different opinion? Paul is convinced that God will bring them round eventually to his point of view. This remarkable tolerance of the opinions of others on an important point is highly significant for Paul's concept of the role of authority in a transforming community. Transformation cannot be achieved by regimentation. The function of authority must be to inspire, that is, to present the christian ideal in such a way that its appeal cannot be mistaken. This cannot be done by words alone. In its plenitude the call of God is a person ('the call of God in Christ Jesus', 3 : 14). To be effective in regard to those who did not walk with Christ on earth it must be transmitted to them as incarnated in a human personality. This tremendous responsibility Paul accepted by proposing his own life as an example to be imitated (3 : 17; 4 : 9). 'Become imitators of me as I am the imitator of Christ' (1 Cor 11 : 1). In his absence the Philippians are to imitate those who live as he does. Here Paul clearly shows his awareness of the need of the average christian for a living symbol of the ideal to which he has committed himself. Unless one or two individuals in the community have this quality, the life of the community disintegrates, and inevitably an effort is made to maintain the ideal by legislation.

1. How closely do present day christian communities correspond to the ideal outlined by Paul?

2. Does the current understanding of the role of authority in the church correspond to that of Paul?

3. Do we have a better language today for expressing the difference between life in the 'flesh' and life in the 'spirit'?

Colossians

Jerome Murphy-O'Connor

Introduction

The epistle to the Colossians might well be subtitled
'How to handle a crisis'. Paul was a prisoner in Rome at
the time of writing (towards the end of the period 61–
63 AD), and news of a potentially explosive situation in
the church at Colossae had been brought to him. Colossae
is located in the middle of modern Turkey, and although
Paul would have passed not very far away on the great
high road down to Ephesus he had never visited it personally. Consequently he had to deal with a crisis in-
volving people with whom he had no personal relations.

This perhaps explains his approach which, for him, is
extremely diplomatic. He takes a long time to mention
the cause of the trouble, and he showers the Colossians
with assurances of his esteem. He is so discreet that it is
not at all easy to determine exactly what caused the disturbance. It appears, however, that a number of itinerant
preachers had come to Colossae, and that the ideas they
proclaimed were exerting a definite fascination on the
young community. On the practical level of external observances these were fundamentally Jewish, but linked
with them was a certain amount of speculation concerning the role of angels in the salvation of mankind.
And it was really this that touched Paul on the raw, because it implicitly diminished the role of Christ, and

because it pushed redemption out of history and into the cloudy realms of theory.

His reaction was at once polemic and positive, because the line he took was to try to give the Colossians a more profound understanding of what they already possessed. If they fully appreciated its richness, variety and wisdom they would not be tempted by more facile doctrines. Thus the crisis was, for Paul, an occasion to penetrate more deeply the mystery and meaning of Christ. This is why the theology of this letter is somewhat different from that of Corinthians or Romans. Paul's thought has moved forward. Hence, if it has no other value, Colossians is an object lesson as to how one should react in the crisis situation through which the church is passing today.

Book list

1. *Jerusalem Bible.* Useful notes and index of theological themes, but the translation is far inferior to that of the RSV.

2. *The Epistle to the Colossians and to Philemon,* C. F. D. Moule. Based on the Greek text, but the reader who does not know Greek can, with a little ingenuity, draw material of tremendous value from this deceptively simple commentary.

3. *The Body,* John A. T. Robinson. Rather difficult reading, but very rewarding, particularly for the concepts of 'flesh' and 'body'.

1
The address
Col 1:1–2

The Pauline epistles are *letters,* and for their correct understanding it is important to recognise that they are the work of an individual standing at a fixed point in history. They are coloured by his moods and preoccupations. They reflect his problems and the circumstances in which he found himself. They echo, faintly at times, the other voices that competed for the attention of his readers. The personality of Paul even breaks through the rather rigid epistolary etiquette of the first century. Brevity was a strict rule, particularly in the self-designation of the writer. At the beginning of his career Paul conformed to this convention (cf 1 Thess 1 : 1; 2 Thess 1 : 1), but later broke with it to include a phrase underlining the authority accruing to him from his mission, eg 'apostle of Christ Jesus by the will of God'. The significance of this is that Paul obviously intended his letters to have a normative value.

Greater latitude was permitted the writer in the designation of the recipients, and the address varied according to the type of relationship between the two parties, their social standing, etc. Paul made full use of this freedom, and from the way he phrases the address we very often catch a hint of his mood as he writes. The tone in 1 and 2 Thess and 1 and 2 Cor is official and dry, but it does not convey the same impression as the stern 'to the churches of Galatia' which prepares us for the exposition of the sorry state of that church. Philemon provides a vivid contrast, for Paul's deep affection for this individual is very evident. Between these two extremes we have a group of three letters (Phil, Rom, and Col) addressed 'to the saints'. 'Dedicated' would perhaps be a better translation, because the underlying Hebrew term *kadosh* does not primarily connote personal virtue, but separation from the profane in virtue of complete consecration to God. Paul is speaking to those who have experienced a 'call' (cf Rom 1 : 7) to total commitment. In this epistle he further qualifies them as 'faithful' (= 'steadfast'). This is the first hint of trouble at Colossae, because the implication is that some members of the church have fallen away. And it is doubly significant. Not only does the delicacy of the allusion indicate how much Paul has mellowed since the days of Galatians (the first explicit reference to trouble at Colossae comes in 2 : 8), but its presence provides a valuable clue to the interpretation of the sections on Christ and the apostolate which take up the rest of ch 1. We must assume that they were relevant to the crisis situation, and that in thought, and even in expression, they were conditioned by the contradictory error.

1. Why, and in what sense, can a letter written to meet a specific need in the first century be considered normative today?

2. In what sense is the christian separated from the world by his response to the divine call?

3. Our understanding of the notions sacred and pro-fane is in evolution. To what extent can we accept Paul's notion that consecration and commitment involve de-tachment from the profane? To what extent are the categories 'sacred' and 'profane' valid?

2

Thanksgiving and prayer
Col 1:3–11

An expression of gratitude occurs immediately after the
greeting in every extant Pauline epistle except Gal. Here
it is motivated by two virtues of the Colossians: faith
and love.

As always in Paul, 'faith' is not simply acceptance, but
a positive orientation of the entire personality founded
on a decision to commit oneself to God's love as incarnated in the person of Christ. Here this faith is qualified
by the words 'in Christ Jesus'. This phrase occurs very
frequently in the pauline letters and in the most varied
contexts. It is therefore one of his fundamental ideas.
Yet it utterly defies definite interpretation. What Paul
is groping towards can only be grasped in the context of
his whole christology whose basic notion is that of our
'in-corporation' into Christ. The best image is perhaps
that of an electromagnetic forcefield. Certainly to understand the phrases here as indicating merely the object of
our dedication is to underestimate the depth of his
thought.

This epistle never speaks of 'love' as directed to God.
Love is mentioned in five passages, and the relationship
implied is always horizontal, never vertical:

On the divine level: 1 : 13.
On the human level: 1 : 4, 8; 2 : 2; 3 : 14.

In the latter series the emphasis is on the unitive effect of love. This might be expected in view of the hint that Paul has already given us regarding the divided state of the community at Colossae. 3 : 14 is particularly clear and forceful. 'Put on love, which binds everything together in perfect harmony'. The expression 'put on' is peculiar, and can only be explained in the context of other passages where this terminology is found, especially those where Paul exhorts his readers to 'put on Christ' (Gal 3 : 27; Rom 13 : 14). In Gal 3 : 27 this putting on of Christ is related explicitly to baptism, and it is very likely that the terminology was suggested by the symbolic value seen in the clothing of the believer in new garments after his immersion. This love, therefore, is for Paul a specifically christian phenomenon, because it is intimately related to the Christ-event. Note too that in 1 : 17 Christ is presented as the cohesive principle of the church. Elsewhere it is made clear that Christ is the model of this love. 'Walk in love as Christ loved us, and gave himself up for us, a fragrant offering and sacrifice to God' (Eph 5 : 2). The 'and' in this text is explicative. The 'loving' is the surrender of self on behalf of the other. The only affirmation of love compatible with the following of Christ is a dynamic one (cf Mt 7 : 21), a statement expressed not in words but in deeds.

This faith and this love are next associated with 'hope', but not quite in the way we would expect, because hope is not the virtue, but the object of hope, ie that which we hope for. The effect is to make the exercise of faith and love dependent on a future reward. This will appear shocking only to those who have a less realistic view of human nature than Paul, because there is a measure of self-interest in our most altruistic actions. An 'I-Thou' relationship is of its very nature reciprocal. In giving we receive, and it is this that makes giving on a still deeper level possible. Thus even though Paul stresses the future quality of the reward, it is clear that it is to some extent a present reality also. He cannot see total fulfilment as possible within the limits of existence as we now know it. Yet it is to this that man aspires. Hence he affirms his faith in a new mode of existence in which it will be possible.

He knows this through revelation. Hence he passes from the idea of this new dimension of existence to the means whereby the Colossians became aware of it: the preaching of Epaphras. But for Paul the preacher appears to be of less importance than the word itself. This is quite consistent with his position in other letters, eg 'I am not ashamed of the gospel since it is a divine power for the salvation of every believer' (Rom 1:16; cf 1 Thess 2:13; 2 Thess 3:1; 1 Cor 1:18). Here an image is used, a tree or a plant, and the idea evoked is not simply power, but power-in-action. The use of the verb 'to be' with a present participle emphasises the continuity of present action. The power of the word of God is known and recognised in the change it is bringing about in the community at Colossae. This is the guarantee that Paul offers against the fear of the Colossians that what they received was in some way imperfect. Remember that the section under consideration is a latent polemic against those who were disturbing the community by suggesting (at the very least) that the doctrine it has accepted needed to be 'supplemented'. Hence the emphasis that what the Colossians 'have heard before (the arrival of the false teachers)' was *'the truth'*. It is their new teachers who are out of agreement with the common gospel.

In 1 : 9 Paul's attention switches from the past to the future, and although he is obviously very uneasy about the situation we feel his optimism, and the real confidence that he has in his readers. His whole approach is based on the assumption of their goodwill. Hence the entirely positive tone of the liturgically cadenced petition that he offers for them. He begs God to grant them (i) a sensitiveness to God's will consisting in a grasp of what is spiritually valuable, (ii) the overflow of this knowledge into external activity, and (iii) the strength required to do this.

A number of commentators object to the translation 'to be filled with knowledge', but its very literalness is necessary to bring out the nuance of Paul's thought which would seem to be that if the Colossians are filled with a profound awareness of God's demands upon them they will be less likely to crave merely human speculation (cf 2 : 8) which is the root of all the trouble in the community. There seems to be a further polemic thrust in the emphasis laid on the 'spiritual' quality of this knowledge. Behind this lies the pauline distinction between 'flesh' and 'spirit'. These are not two substances. 'Flesh' has two principal connotations in pauline theology. One is neutral and simply indicates man's facticity as existing in the world. The other is pejorative and indicates a mode of being in which man has orientated himself to the visible and the tangible, in which his true self is lost and scattered in the instrumental world of things and in the depersonalised world of mass-existence (cf Rom 12 : 2). 'Spirit' is also a mode of being, but one in which man is not dependent on the world for his understanding of himself. He sees himself as a creature, and is orientated to God. This is the result of the decision of faith made possible by Christ. Given absolute fidelity to this commitment, Paul is confident that man will have the wisdom and insight to perceive the demands that God is making upon him.

This awareness, however, is not knowledge in the Greek sense of a cool, detached, speculative regard. For Paul one does not know the truth unless one lives it. Hence his stress on the activity that must result if this knowledge is to be real. No more than in the previous verse does he go into detail as to the type of activity that he expects. In his mind positive directives were only for those who did not have the maturity to think for themselves in function of their basic commitment to God in Christ. To those who are mature he simply says: 'Whatever is true, whatever is honourable, whatever is just, whatever is pure, whatever is lovely, whatever is gracious, if there is any excellence, if there is anything worthy of praise, think about these things' (Phil 4:8).

This is a deceptively easy principle to live by. But Paul was fully aware of the courage and patience required if it is taken seriously. It is extremely difficult to remain open to God, because this openness necessarily involves a radical honesty with oneself, and self-knowledge is painful. However, the quest for authenticity should not be characterised by tension or anxiety, but by serenity and joy. This is so because Paul was convinced that man is not left to his own resources. He does not have to resign himself to a struggle in loneliness. The prayer uttered by Paul in these three verses (1:9–11) is based on the conviction that God does intervene in history, and that he does aid those who trust in him.

1. Can the power of the word of God be separated from the witness of those who have been transformed by it?

2. Is it possible to suggest some contemporary equivalents for the 'spirit-flesh' terminology employed by Paul?

3. How is divine aid given in the quest for authenticity?

4. What should be the role of positive directives in the christian community?

5. What means can be used by church leaders to foster the maturity which will permit christians to live out their commitment to Christ responsibly?

6. What are the implications of Paul's horizontally directed relations in christian love?

3

Conversion
Col 1:12–14

Christian joy is not based exclusively, or even primarily, on the hope of divine aid in the future. Its roots lie deep in the past, in the experience of transformation or conversion. As the title 'Father' given to God indicates, this is essentially the discovery and affirmation of a relationship. To call God 'Father' as Paul does (cf Gal 4 : 6; Rom 8 : 15) is fundamentally to bear witness to the experience of a relationship in which both God and man have their respective roles. In the present passage only the former is stressed, but this must be balanced by other texts which present the reverse side of the coin, eg 'They themselves report . . . how you turned to God from idols, to serve a living and true God' (1 Thess 1 : 9). These two perspectives are not contradictory or mutually exclusive, because, as Bultmann points out, 'Faith is the work of God in so far as the grace which comes from him first makes possible the human decision, so that his decision itself can be understood only as God's gift, without on that account losing its character as decision' (*Theology of the* NT I, London 1965, 330). Paul's stress on the divine initiative may be due to the experience of his own conversion, and there are a striking number of contacts between our present passage and Paul's reference to this event in his defence before Agrippa in Acts 26 : 18. None the less there must be some element of genuine decision, because otherwise man would lose his distinctively human character and be reduced to the level of an object or automaton. This should not be understood as if decision were the only element in faith—understanding and obedience are also essential—but it is important to keep in mind that in faith man is active and not merely a passive recipient, and this is most easily recognised if the decision aspect is brought to the fore.

Paul uses the image of 'light' and 'darkness' to describe the before and after of conversion. This was a common theme in the old testament (eg Is 9 : 2), and it would be difficult to find any religion in which this obvious metaphor was ignored. Paul, however, penetrates a little more deeply into the problem, by adding the precision that conversion is a passage from one condition of obedience to another, from an arbitrary tyranny (*exousia*) to a well-ordered sovereignty (*basileia*). In each case, however, man is subject to a power outside himself. This idea is somewhat more developed in Rom 6 : 12–23, where it is clear that if man is subject it is because he has freely yielded his allegiance: 'Do you not know that if you yield yourselves to any one as obedient slaves, you are slaves of the one whom you obey, either of sin, which leads to death, or of obedience, which leads to righteousness?' (6 : 16). For Paul, as for the whole new testament, no neutrality was possible in respect of God. Man could and always, in fact, did make a choice either for the creator or for the creature (cf Rom 1 : 18–32). What is the power to which man is subject if he chooses the latter? There is no imperative reason why 'power of darkness' should be interpreted as a personal being, although in view of 2 : 15 this position could be argued. In the light of Rom 1 it is possible to conceive of the realm of darkness as the sphere constituted by man's own vices. Through repetition they constitute a pattern of existence from which unaided he finds it impossible to break away. Hence he needs to be rescued. By equating this redemption with forgiveness of sins Paul firmly underlines the essentially moral dimension of the images he employs.

Paul presents this forgiveness as related to the Father's love for his Son, Christ. It is in virtue of our solidarity ('in whom') with the latter that we become the recipients of this love. Thus, very neatly, Paul brings Christ to the centre of the stage, and the next section will focus explicitly on his role both in creation and in salvation.

1. What is man's role in conversion?

2. What is God's role?

3. What role does decision play in the lives of those baptised as infants? Should infant baptism be reconsidered?

4

The christological hymn
Col 1:15-20

The hymnic character of this section is generally recognised, and there is agreement that we have to do with a
two-strophe hymn depicting the cosmological and soteriological roles of Christ. It is likely that this hymn was
chanted in liturgical assembly by a community before
being incorporated by Paul into this letter. We have an
allusion to such an activity on the part of the community
in 3:16, 'May the word of Christ dwell in you in rich
abundance, (i) in all wisdom teaching and admonishing
each other with psalms and hymns and spiritual songs,
(ii) in thankfulness singing in your hearts to God'. In
this passage Paul has in mind a double manifestation of
the power of the gospel (cf 1:6) which has taken
possession of the community. An intense sentiment of
gratitude (cf 1:12) finds expression in song which in turn
serves to deepen the faith of the community.

The primitive church had no ready-made theology.
The fact of Jesus was given, but much reflection was
necessary to penetrate its meaning, and to discover ways
of expressing in human language the mystery of Christ.
This effort was guided by the Holy Spirit under whose
impulse the church is continually being guided into the
whole truth' (Jn 16:13). It is reasonable to believe that

some of these new insights into the significance of Christ found their first expression, or their expanded development, in charismatic utterances couched in hymnic form ('*spiritual* songs', cf 1 Cor 14:26). Such chants had a definite didactic value, and the seal of orthodoxy was set on the insights they embodied by their adoption by the community as an expression of its faith.

The structure of the present hymn has been disturbed by additions made by Paul but there is little agreement as to the number and extent of these additions, and the following arrangement is put forward tentatively.

The original hymn

Who is the image of the invisible God
First-born of all creation
For in him were created all things
And all things through him and to him have been created.

Who is the beginning
First-born from the dead
For in him dwells all the fullness
And through him all things were reconciled to him.

It will be noted that the pattern of the first strophe is repeated in the second, the first line corresponding to the first, the second to the second, and so on. This is too clear to be anything but intentional. This hymn exhibits close literary and doctrinal affinities with previous pauline letters, and if it was not originally composed by Paul on another occasion, it must be the work of a charismatic deeply imbued with pauline theology. It has been well argued that the hymn is most appropriately situated in the context of a baptismal liturgy. The verses immedi-

ately preceding concern conversion which is per-
fected in submission to the rite of baptism, and the
balance between creation and re-creation achieved by
the hymn is significant in view of Paul's concept of baptism as a new creation (cf 2 Cor 5 : 17). If this suggestion
is correct we have here an insight into Paul's strategy in
this letter. His object is to recall his readers to their
original commitment by evoking a confession made on
the occasion of their baptism.

The hymn as adapted by Paul

Who is the image of the invisible God
First-born of all creation
For in him were created all things
    in heaven and on earth
    visible and invisible
    whether thrones or dominions
    or principalities or powers
All things through him and to him have been
    created.

And he himself is before all things and all things in him
    consist
And he himself is the head of the body, the church

Who is the beginning
First-born from the dead
    that he might in everything himself become pre-
    eminent
For in him he willed all the fullness to dwell
And through him to reconcile all things to him
    making peace by the blood of his cross through
    him
    whether those on earth or those in heaven

The italicised portions are the Pauline additions, and as we shall see they draw out implications of the hymn that are specially relevant for the situation at Colossae. Between the two strophes Paul has inserted a conclusion to the first, and an introduction to the second.

Col 1:15–17. Christ and creation

The human mind advances in knowledge by relating the new and unknown to the categories it already possesses. Thus when the first christians, under the sign of the resurrection, began to reflect on the mystery of Christ, they struggled to relate him to categories with which they were already familiar. One has only to read the new testament to realise what a variety of categories they had. The old testament, in particular, provided an inexhaustible reservoir, and it was supplemented by the writings of the intertestamental period. The author of this hymn was no exception, but his insight into the role of Christ was so profound, so all-embracing, that the better known categories of messiah, Son of God, Son of Man, etc, did not seem adequate to his purpose. Hence he turned to the sapiential literature and in the theme of wisdom he found the concept and the terminology he needed. A close reading of Job 28, Ps 33, Prov 8, Sir 24, and Wis 7 is indispensable to the understanding of what follows. This emerges clearly from a simple listing of the parallels shown opposite.

Wisdom is at once subordinate to God, anterior to all other creatures in time, and superior to them in dignity. In her God contemplated the design of the universe—'when he willed to give weight to the wind, and measured out the waters with a gauge, when he made the laws and

rules for the rain, and mapped a route for the thunder-
claps to follow, then he had it (wisdom) before his eyes'
(Job 28 : 25–27).

Christ	*Wisdom*
Who is the image of the invisible God	The pure emanation of the glory of the Almighty . . . the reflection of eternal light, the untarnished mirror of his active power, the image of his goodness (Wis 7 : 25–26).
First-born of all creation.	The Lord created me at the beginning of his work (Prov 8 : 22).
For in him were created all things	The Lord by wisdom founded the earth (Prov 3 : 19). I was beside him like a master-workman (Prov 8 : 30).
And he himself is before all things	Before all other things wisdom was created (Sir 1 : 4). Over every people and nation I have held sway (Sir 24 : 6–9).
All things in him consist.	All things hold together by means of his [God's] word (Sir 43 : 26, cf 24 : 5—I came forth from the mouth of the Most High).

The whole of creation is, as it were, permeated by the
creative wisdom of God. These passages (whose thought
is also reflected in the prologue to the fourth gospel, Jn
1 : 1–18) are best understood as hymns of praise expressive of awe at the thought of the unique creator of so
many marvels. This view of reality is essentially optimistic. The world is not a frightening place into which
man is thrown as into a sea of alien being where chance
is king and purpose a myth. It is a place of wonder and
beauty, because it is viewed in a perspective that sees
unity of origin and purpose. For the OT writers this per-

spective was given by wisdom; for the author of this hymn it is provided by Christ. Christ for him is all in all, and he makes no distinction between the pre-existent word and the incarnate Jesus. He is a figure whose influence is so all-pervasive now that it must have been at work since the beginning of time. Thus a role in creation is attributed to Christ, and the wisdom literature provides the terminology to express it. Paul draws out the implications of 'all things' (1 : 16a) in order to make it clear that the angelic beings on whom the false teachers laid such stress were conceived in function of Christ, and were, in consequence, inferior to him. It is difficult to say whether we can attribute to Paul a real belief in the existence of these beings. His essential point, as will appear later, is that these beings certainly cannot fulfil the role that the heretics attribute to them.

There is no parallel in the sapiential literature to the striking assertion that Christ embodies the finality of the world. It is useful to compare 1 Cor 8 : 6—the brackets indicate words inserted to clarify the translation, because the Greek uses no verbs: 'For us [there is but] one God, the Father, from whom [come] all things, and to whom we [go]. And one Lord, Jesus Christ, through whom [come] all things, and through him we [go].' God is the Alpha and the Omega of everything that is (Is 44 : 6; Rev 1 : 8, 17), the source of its being and perfection, the end towards which it tends and for which it was made. This is a commonplace in any theistic concept of the world, but how are we to reconcile it with the role attributed to Christ in the hymn? One possibility is to see the hymn as an implicit affirmation of the divinity of Christ. This approach gives its full value to the assertion that Christ is the 'image' of God, because in semitic thought an

image was conceived as the projection or exteriorisation
of the being of the original. Another possibility is to see
Christ as the perfect realisation of God's design for his
creation, since in him creator and creature are joined in
total harmony. In this perspective Christ, as it were, pro-
grammes the true destiny of the world.

Col 1:18–20. Christ and re-creation

With 1 : 18 we turn to the second panel of the diptych,
and move from the material (or cosmological) into the
moral (or soteriological) order. It is with this dimension
that Paul is particularly concerned.

The introduction of the church at this point (1 : 18a)
disturbs the equilibrium of the two strophes, and it is
best to consider it as an introduction to the second
strophe. The gradual development of the theme of the
church as the body of Christ which can be traced through
Gal 2 : 26–29, 1 Cor 6 : 13–17, 10 : 14–21, 12 : 12–27 and
Rom 12 : 45 here reaches its climax. 'The body' has become an accepted designation of the universal church,
and by the introduction of the theme of 'head' the whole
Christ is more adequately distinguished from the individual Christ. In this epistle 'head' is used with two
distinct connotations: (i) dignity and authority (here and
2 : 10), and (ii) source of vitality (2 : 19). An allusion to
the former is to be found in the idea of preeminence, and
to the latter in the title 'the beginning'. Thus the introduction is perfectly adapted to the theme of the second
strophe which is concerned with the action of Christ in
the sphere of salvation which is the church.

Some authors prefer the rendering 'the principle' instead of 'the beginning'. This is possibly a little too ab-

stract to be truly biblical, but it has the advantage of bringing out the idea that Christ has a real influence on all that happens subsequent to this beginning. The background here is again Prov 8:22. Compare Prov 8:35 ('The man who finds me [wisdom] finds life'), with the title 'author of life' given to Christ in Acts 4:15.

Christ is also termed 'first-born from the dead' in Rev 1:4, and an analogous idea is to be found in Rom 8 where Paul says that God predestined those whom he foreknew to be conformed to the image of his Son 'in order that he might be the first-born among many brethren' (8:29). The primary reference here is to the resurrection of Christ, but an allusion to the spiritual resurrection effected in baptism is not to be excluded, because we are conformed to the image of the Son by putting on Christ, which is an effect of the sacrament of baptism. These two aspects are closely connected, because it is a characteristic of pauline theology that the resurrection marked a new beginning both for Christ and for humanity. Here the stress is on preeminence in dignity and authority, because of Paul's polemic against the heretics, but elsewhere he stresses that it was through the resurrection that Christ was '*constituted* Son of God in power' (Rom 1:4), and '*became* a life-giving spirit' (1 Cor 15:45). In both these texts the emphasis is on the advantages accruing to humanity—a theme that will appear in 1:20. There, however, Paul has the passion in mind, but we should remember that the writers of the new testament did not draw the clear distinction between passion and resurrection that we are inclined to do. They were but two facets of a unique mighty act of God.

1:19 has rightly been characterised as one of the most obscure and disputed verses in the pauline letters. It is

intended to answer the question: why was Christ the
first to be raised from the dead? The same question is
answered in another way in the pauline insertion in 1 : 18d,
ie in terms of pre-eminence. The answer given here is
on a much more fundamental level, and the key point
is obviously the term 'fulness' (*plērōma*). It is understood
by some to mean the church, but nothing in the context
supports this interpretation. The majority of scholars
understand it as the plenitude of divinity—and this view
is reflected in the gratuitous addition 'of God' in the RSV.
Ultimately, however, this opinion is based on the technical value of *plērōma* in gnostic texts written much later
than this epistle. However, gnosticism was not the only
philosophy to use this concept. The stoics conceived the
cosmos as a unified diversity in which the divine spirit
compenetrated material reality, 'filling' it with its universal presence and in turn 'being filled' with it. It is
impossible to see this materialistic immanentism reflected in this hymn, but purified of its pantheistic asso-
ciations it rejoins the old testament theme of the close
bond between creator and creation, eg 'Do I not fill
heaven and earth?—it is Yahweh who speaks' (Jer 23 :
24; cf Is 6 : 3, Ps 50 : 12, 72 : 19, etc). There is here a sense
of the divine omnipresence which easily lent itself to expression in stoic terms when this philosophy came into
contact with biblical thought, eg 'The spirit of the Lord
fills the whole world' (Wis 1 : 7). In this perspective
plērōma is the plenitude of being, and englobes both the
divinity and the material world. Understood in this sense,
this verse takes up the thought of the corresponding line
in the first strophe (1 : 16a) while at the same time opening up new perspectives. This interpretation makes it
clear that the subject of 'willed' is 'God' (understood).

The following verse (1 : 20) also depends on 'God willed', and it is here that we must seek for the meaning of the mysterious indwelling affirmed of Christ in the previous one. In the old testament man had to take the first steps to reconcile himself with a wrathful God (cf 2 Mac 1 : 5, 7 : 33, 8 : 23). Paul, on the other hand, stresses that the initiative lies exclusively with God whose immense love (Eph 2 : 4–6) moves him to establish harmonious relations with a humanity whose inherent tendency is to withdraw from him. It is by reconciling a sin-divided cosmos through Christ that God makes it to dwell in him. This reconciliation of the cosmos (note the repetition of 'all things') is a very mysterious thing. It is not possible in any real sense to speak of purely material entities as affected by sin, for sin implies a moral dimension that they by definition lack. If it is truly a question of reconciliation man, the microcosmos, must stand in the forefront of the author's thought. It is he who creates the need for reconciliation, and the work of reconciliation is focused in and through him. To understand this it is necessary to appreciate the old testament view of man and the world in which he lived. Things had their own built-in finalities and needs, but man could distort their orientation by using them to augment a false sense of self-sufficiency, or to increase the destructiveness of his sins. Thus for Leviticus the very land breathes a sigh of relief and resumes its interior rhythm when the sinful Israelites are driven into exile (Lev 26 : 33–35). In a somewhat different form the same idea appears in Rom 8 : 20–21, 'It was not for any fault on the part of creation that it was made unable to attain its purpose, it was made so; but creation still retains the hope of being freed, like us, from decadence'. The rather poetic imagery of these texts embodies a profound insight into the fundamental harmony of creation. Inevitably, then, man's sin was seen as upsetting the delicate balance of the whole, and his reconciliation with God was viewed as having a cosmic dimension. By repeating 'through him' Paul firmly underlines the mediatory role of Christ in this reconciliation. In his life, and particularly in his death, he concretised the Father's love in such a way as to make it almost palpable to man. It is in responding to this love that man is reconciled. But the only adequate response is a life imbued with love of the same quality, because only through love as lived can the harmony of reality be restored.

1. In describing the central role of Christ the author drew on categories found in the wisdom literature. Today are other categories possible and/or desirable?

2. Is the description of Christ's relationship to the creative act a myth?

3. What grounds do we have to share the author's optimistic outlook on the world? Without his perspective is it possible to hope?

4. Was the construction of the atom bomb a distortion of the finality of material creation?

5

Participation of the Colossians in salvation Col 1:21–23

In this section Paul descends rather abruptly from the general to the particular, and concerns himself with the 'once' and 'now' of the situation of the Colossians. He touches on the 'once'—their state before they knew Christ —only in order to highlight the 'now'.

Once the Colossians were 'strangers and enemies through your evil thoughts and deeds'. Obviously it is a question of their alienation from God, and Paul makes it quite clear that this state is a result not of their status as gentiles ('strangers and enemies', cf Eph 2 : 12), but of personal sin. He will return to this theme in 2 : 20 and 3 : 9–10.

Now, however, they have been reconciled with God. No longer do they look on him as a judge, but as a father (1 : 2). How has this change been brought about? Paul's answer here is very schematic, and it needs to be completed by what he will say in 2 : 9 f. He first touches on the role of Christ, and then on that of the Colossians.

We have already touched on the pejorative sense that the word 'flesh' can have in pauline theology (cf pp 160–61). This is not implied in the unusual phrase 'body of flesh' where the term simply has the effect of stressing the

physical character of Christ. The point is not to distinguish the individual Christ from his mystical body,
the church. The terminology 'mystical body' was coined
much later, and was originally a designation of the
eucharist. Paul's intention was almost certainly polemic,
and the redundant phrase is directed against the false
teachers who may have attributed a share in the work
of redemption to incorporeal angels. This Paul em-
phatically denies because, as beings without bodies, they
could not share man's way of being, and in consequence
could do nothing to reverse the situation in which sinful
man found himself. Christ, on the other hand, was a man,
and the change that he wrought in the human situation
was effected from within. It could not have been imposed
from the outside. This is because sin, being a personal
attitude, cannot simply be blotted out. It must be pun-
ished or expiated. The death of Christ was an act of
complete expiation in which men shared in virtue of
their solidarity with him. The ultimate finality of
Christ's act was that men should appear before God not
as 'strangers and enemies', but 'holy, faultless and ir-
reproachable'.

However, to share a common human condition is not
sufficient to establish this solidarity with Christ, because
while he does for us what we could not do for ourselves,
we for our part must do what he will not do for us. And
this is precisely our recognition of what he has done and
continues to do for us, namely, faith. This is our decision.
Paul insists on loyalty to the decision already taken. It is
a commitment that should exercise a continuing influence on one's whole life, imparting to it a quality of
stability and steadfastness. He is thinking obviously of

the shaky state of the community at Colossae, which does not quite know whom or what to believe.

1. How are we led to commit ourselves to Christ?

2. Paul seems to imply that to doubt is unchristian. Can this be reconciled with the state of the church today?

3. How are we to understand the ambiguity that redemption, accomplished once for all and fully by Christ, is nevertheless an on-going process?

6

The role of the apostle
Col 1:24–2:5

The specifically polemic part of the epistle runs from
2 : 6 to 3 : 4, and Paul's criticisms there are rather pointed.
He was fully aware that these could be received in a way
which would only make the situation worse. Hence he
does his best to dispose the Colossians to docile acceptance by underlining (i) his divine commission and the
zeal with which he carries it out (1 : 24–29), and (ii) his
solicitude for the churches of the Lycus valley and the
confidence he has in them.

Col 1:24–29

The wealth of ideas packed into these few verses is typical
of Paul. His mind was so active, and so single in its commitment that unique insights flash out at us continually.
For example, he speaks of his work as being a 'fulfilment
of the word of God' (1 : 25—RSV mistranslates in rendering 'to make the word of God fully known'). The reference is obviously to his preaching (1 : 27), but the curious
terminology indicates that his mind has run over the sur-
face of several ideas which in his urgency have been
blurred together. Basically there is the idea that in acting
as he does Paul is fulfilling a commission entrusted to
him. He is fully conscious that he is only an agent (cf 1

Cor 3 : 10, 4 : 1–2); that he does not act on his own authority or in virtue of his own power (1 : 29). His whole
raison d'être comes from a unique relationship to Christ.
But just as Christ is the beginning, so is he also the end,
because Paul's function is to realise a presence of Christ
among the gentiles (1 : 27). In preaching the 'mystery'
(1 : 26) which is God's salvific plan for humanity focused
on Christ, Paul brings it to fulfilment (in Greek *logos* can
mean both 'word' and 'plan').

Paul, however, was fully aware that words alone are
not sufficient to bring men to accept Christ. The affirmation that leads to faith must be much more deeply rooted
in the whole person. Hence Paul evokes his sufferings.
It is these that give his words validity as expressions of
an unshakable conviction. The first part of 1 : 24 presents
no difficulty, but the second part ('to complete what is
lacking in the afflictions of Christ') is one of the peren-
nial problems of pauline exegesis. The difficulty arises
because of the multiple value of the genitive in Greek.
Theoretically the phrase 'the afflictions of Christ' can
have four meanings: (i) afflictions borne for Christ,
(ii) afflictions like those of Christ, (iii) afflictions undergone by Christ, (iv) afflictions borne by the members of
Christ's body. Which did Paul intend? The immediate
context affords no clues. Hence we must try to determine
which meaning accords best with the theology of suffering that he elaborated in previous letters. This might
seem a rather vague criterion, but the sentence with
which we are concerned is inserted almost as an aside
into the development of Paul's thought, and it is unlikely that he would introduce a completely new idea in
such a casual way. Three passages merit consideration,
Rom 8 : 17–18, 2 Cor 1 : 4–4, 4 : 8–10, because they reveal

the same basic thought pattern as 1:24. Paul speaks first
of suffering in its concrete reality, and then reveals its
theological value in virtue of his fundamental concept of
the christian's life in Christ. This emerges very clearly if
the key phrases of the four texts are set out in parallel.

Rom 8:18 'the present sufferings'	8:17 'we suffer with him'
2 Cor 1:4 'in all our affliction'	1:5 'the sufferings of Christ'
2 Cor 4:8 'we are afflicted in every way'	4:10 'the dying of Christ'
Col 1:24a 'my sufferings'	1:24b 'the afflictions of Christ'

The one conclusion that emerges is that it is very probable that here as in the other passages the 'afflictions of
Christ' means Paul's sufferings as viewed in the perspective of the close union between the risen Christ and
him in whom his spirit is active. 'Christ' then is not the
historical Jesus, but the Lord as living in his members.

It is in this perspective, therefore, that we must seek
the meaning of the phrase 'to complete what is lacking'.
The Greek verb used (*antanapleroō*) gives us a further
clue, because it implies a duality which excludes the
complete identification of the sufferings of Paul with
those of the whole Christ. This suggests that others also
have a role to play in completing the measure of suffering of the whole Christ. But in what sense? The answer
is indicated by Paul's assertion that his sufferings are 'for
the sake of his body, the church'. Until the end of time
the church will be imperfect, in the sense that it must
continually develop both intensively and extensively (cf

Eph 4 : 10–13). In virtue of their basic commitment
solemnised in baptism all christians are called to contribute to narrowing the gap between the actual and the
potential, the real and the ideal. This they do simply by
'living the truth in love' (Eph 4 : 15), which inescapably
involves suffering. Pain is always a condition of growth.
In this perspective, Paul is saying in effect that although
he suffers, this is no more than any christian worthy of
the name would do. This interpretation is confirmed by
Phil 3 : 7–11, where Paul in a reflective mood counts his
blessings. Among them he lists 'experience of the *fellowship* of his [Christ's] sufferings' (3 : 10). His pride is that
his personal sufferings have won him a place in the company of those who are truly other Christs, the men who
bring religion out of the clouds and into real life.

1. What is the essential apostolate?

*2. Why does the christian life when fully lived inescap-
ably involve suffering?*

*3. In the perspective of the second question is there
any justification for special penitential practices?*

Col 2:1–5

Laodicea was the most important city in the Lycus valley,
a position it had taken over from Colossae, its immediate
neighbour. Relations between the two were very close,
and Paul no doubt had reason to fear that the disturbance
in the church at Colossae might also spread to Laodicea.
Hence he orders that this letter be passed on to the
Laodiceans and read publicly in the liturgical assembly
(4 : 16). He further suggests that the Colossians read the
'letter [which will come to you] from Laodicea'. This was

certainly a letter he had addressed to that church, and it
is possibly to be identified with the epistle to the Ephesians. This letter is an expanded synthesis of the new
insights attained by Paul in reacting to the crisis at
Colossae, and its positive explanatory approach would be
the perfect complement to the letter addressed to the
Colossians, in which the polemic overtones are only too
clear.

Paul's care, therefore, was very practical, but it appears
from 2 : 2 that his true 'striving' was essentially prayer,
together with the offering of his sufferings (1 : 24). He
prays that the Colossians may find courage and strength,
and that they may form a close-knit community permeated by love. This supreme virtue becomes crucial at
moments of crisis, because it gives durability to decision.
It is not clear whether Paul hopes that this love will give
a clarity of insight in the present difficult situation. In
any case Paul also prays that the Colossians may possess
'all the riches of assured knowledge'. Polemic overtones
are easy to detect. Paul implicitly contrasts the certitude
they have in the preaching of the gospel with the un-
founded speculation of the false teachers, which he dismisses as simply 'beguiling speech', mere words. The
doctrine they have received is of such a depth and richness that they have no need to seek supplements elsewhere. Christ is the all-sufficient wisdom in which they
have been trained (1 : 27, 3 : 11). This presentation of
Christ as divine wisdom makes explicit what is latent in
the titles of the christological hymn (1 : 15–20).

In 2 : 5 we see a concrete example of what Paul means
by the unitive effects of love. His affection for the communities in his charge was so profound that he felt himself to be spiritually present among them (cf 1 Cor 5 : 3–5,

Phil 1:7). What we have seen so far would suggest that his compliment on the Colossians' good order and stability is pure diplomacy.

1. What is the relationship between love, prayer, and insight?

2. In religious matters does love give insight?

3. What does Paul mean when he says that the knowledge given by the official preaching is all-sufficient?

7

Warning against errors
Col 2:6–3:4

In this section Paul gets down to the real business of the letter, and the introduction (2 : 6–7) foreshadows what is to come. Its structure is typical of a pauline exhortation. A dogmatic indicative is followed by a moral imperative. The former is developed in 2 : 9–15, and the latter in 2 : 16–3 : 4. In Paul's mind ethics and belief were inseparable, because moral activity was that which flowed naturally from the believer's commitment to Christ.

This commitment necessarily involved a clear recognition of who Christ is. Hence the fundamental statement in the indicative: 'You received Christ [as] Jesus the Lord' (2 : 6). The true doctrine of Christ embodies (i) the acceptance of the historical person of *Jesus*—only rarely does Paul use 'Jesus' alone and always in a context which evokes the events of the passion and resurrection; (ii) the recognition of this Jesus as *Lord,* ie as the messianic saviour—as is clear from Rom 1 : 3–4 this was a state that Jesus attained in virtue of his resurrection, which in turn presupposes the passion. It is very likely that the heretics were concentrating on the second aspect to the detriment of the first. If this was in fact the case, then their teaching amounted to a denial of the reality of the incarnation, and in particular of the events conditioned by it. It is reasonable to suppose that the 'word of the cross' was to them nothing but 'folly' (1 Cor 1:18), and unworthy of incorporation into any self-respecting theology of salvation. Christianity without the cross is obviously much more easily assimilated than the authentic doctrine, and this was the temptation that Paul feared.

Since the Colossians originally accepted Christ 'as he is truth in Jesus' (Eph 4:21), they must (2:6b–7—imperative) remain faithful to this belief and live out its consequences. This will have the effect of a progressive deepening of their conviction.

Col 2:8–16. Christ and the christian

In 2:8 we find the first explicit mention of the Colossian heresy. It is a 'philosophy' which Paul characterises as 'empty deceit', because it gives the central place not to Christ but to the 'elements of the world'. In profane literature this phrase means the constituent elements of the physical world—fire, water, air, and earth. It is very doubtful, however, that Paul is here using 'world' in this very material sense. In his theology it is frequently used as a designation not of the universe, but of the sphere of human activity constituted by interpersonal relationships. In this perspective the 'elements' would be the factors that condition human existence without Christ. In the perspective of Rom 7 these would appear to be sin and death, and their ancillaries the flesh and the law (with which angelic powers were closely associated, cf Gal 3:19, Heb 2:2). If this interpretation is correct, 'the elements of the world' is not a formula used by the heretics, but Paul's understanding of the implications of their teaching. While they perhaps did not intend it as such, it amounted to a complete denial of the relevance of Christ. We shall see in the next section that the Colossian heresy was basically Jewish in character, and that to advocate, even implicitly, a return to the regime of the law was, for Paul, to prefer the shadow to the reality (2:17).

For Paul, the central element in any theory of salvation, in fact in any theory of the meaning of human existence, was Christ, because in him was the plenitude of all being. This was the radical source of his authority over all beings, a fortiori, therefore, over the angelic beings on which the false teachers laid such emphasis. Paul, however, does not pursue this negative approach. He is less concerned with crushing the heretics and exposing their pretensions than with revealing to the Colossians the value of what they already possess.

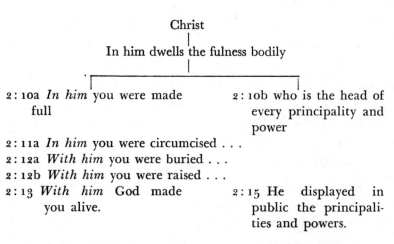

Christ

In him dwells the fulness bodily

2:10a *In him* you were made full

2:10b who is the head of every principality and power

2:11a *In him* you were circumcised . . .
2:12a *With him* you were buried . . .
2:12b *With him* you were raised . . .
2:13 *With him* God made you alive.

2:15 He displayed in public the principalities and powers.

This schematic outline brings to the fore the salient idea of this section. The angelic powers are on the periphery of Paul's thought, and one has the impression that he would not have spoken of them had he not been forced by circumstances to do so, and then he is content to state

that they are inferior to Christ. He is their 'head', as he
is ours, but with a major difference. In the former case
'head' carries only the connotation of authority and dignity, whereas in the latter 'head' is essentially the source
of vital activity (cf 2 : 19). The christian is what he is
because of his union with Christ ('in him/with him').
Hence Paul turns his attention to baptism, the sacrament
by which this union is effected. He first speaks of baptism
as a 'circumcision' (2 : 11). This seems to be because of his
view that the 'flesh' was the avenue whereby sin gained
dominion over man. Jewish circumcision, which was
'made with hands' (Eph 2 : 11), only removed a tiny particle of flesh. Its christian counterpart, baptism, has a much
more radical effect, because by destroying the whole
body-person viewed precisely as 'flesh' (in the prejorative
sense, ie the self as the willing servant of sin) it breaks
completely the tyranny of sin. The complexity of this idea
where the thought seems to be moving on several levels
at once betrays Paul's rabbinic background. In more contemporary terms all he seems to be saying is that baptism
means a radical break with the past with all its habits and
patterns of thought. They are cut off as completely as
the particle of skin in circumcision and are no longer part
of us. This, of course, is not an automatic consequence
of the sacrament. A personal decision is essential, as Paul
suggests in the next verse by the mention of 'faith'.

On the community level faith is expressed by submission to the rite of baptism, which in the time of Paul was
by immersion. Paul never makes the slightest allusion to
the details of the rite, but it was certainly the symbolism
of the immersion that gave him his key insight into the
significance of the event. The descent into the water from

which the believer rises to a new mode of life is at once an end and a beginning. The water evokes the tomb of Christ, and it was but a short step to seeing baptism as a participation in the two events which it links, the passion and resurrection. Baptism means to the individual what these events meant to the whole of humanity.

This dimension is evoked in 2:14, of which the best translation is probably 'Having completely wiped out our bond [to subscribe] to the ordinances, which stood against us; he set it aside nailing it to the cross'. 'Ordinances' is deliberately vague so as to cover both cases, Jews who were bound by the law and gentiles who were bound by their own consciences (Rom 1:32, 2:12–16). For a good example of a 'bond' see Philem 19. Though having signed an undertaking by their very existence as creatures, men had consistently failed to respond to the demands welling up from their nature. This failure God 'blotted out' by the expiatory death of Christ in which we are included by baptism. An IOU cannot be urged against a dead man (cf Rom 7:1). As Professor Moule has remarked, the metaphor is so violent as practically to rupture itself. At least it gives us some idea of what an exciting preacher Paul must have been!

This is confirmed by the next verse, which bears a certain similarity to 2:11. Again the translation is difficult, but a very good case can be made for the following : 'Having divested himself [of his flesh], he boldly displayed in public the principalities and powers, leading them in triumphal procession on the cross'. The dying Jesus like a king divests himself of that 'flesh' which is the tool and medium of the powers of evil, thus reducing them to impotence. Whatever the external appearances the crucifixion was not a failure.

1. Do we feel the desire to make christianity more acceptable? Can this be described as a 'temptation'?

2. What does it mean today to accept Jesus as Lord?

3. How is this acceptance expressed in baptism?

Col 2:16–23. Against false asceticism

External (Jewish) observances with regard to diet and the calendar are no longer of any value. Even the preparatory role that they played with regard to Christ has now ended (Gal 3:24–25). To give them any role in salvation is to live as if one 'still belonged to the world' (2:20). It is obviously not a question here of physical presence in the world. Paul is thinking in terms of authentic and inauthentic existence which he defines exclusively by reference to Christ. Any existence in which Christ is not the fundamental 'reality' (or 'substance', 2:17) is inauthentic. Further on this same contrast is expressed in terms of 'things that are above' and 'things that are on the earth' (3:2). The distinction is not between spiritual and material, but between matters of ultimate concern and trivialities, and again these must be defined in reference to Christ. The practices and regulations (2:21) proposed by the false teachers were obviously conceived by them as having a value in and of themselves. And it is as such that Paul repudiates them so vigorously. He is not opposed to external observances as such, but to a materialistic type of superstitious ritualism.

1. What practices in the church today fall under Paul's condemnation?

2. How can external observances be related to authentic existence in Paul's sense?

3. What difference is there between the Jewish practices condemned by Paul and similar christian practices? Is there any, or are such things accretions which all religions are liable to collect?

4. There is a strong tendency in all the churches today to abandon old ascetic and devotional practices. Does this involve a loss, and if so how can it be made good?

8

The practical implications of faith
Col 3:5–4:6

It is characteristic of the pauline letters generally that they fall into two parts, which are categorised as dogmatic and moral, and Colossians is no exception. The reason for this is found in the paradox which is the best expression of pauline ethics: become what you are! We read, for example, in 3:3 'You have died' and in 3:5 'Put to death therefore'. Fundamentally this is just another instance of Paul's realism. By the decision of faith man may change the basic orientation of his life, but he can never free himself from his past. The living out of his commitment is therefore a struggle, and Paul endeavours to aid him on two levels. First by deepening his appreciation of the true nature of his commitment and what it has done to him, and secondly by indicating a number of ways in which this commitment should be realised in daily life.

The struggle between past and present is expressed here in function of the contrast 'old man—new man'. Ideally this metamorphosis is instantaneous, and takes place at the moment of baptism, as the terminology 'putting on' and 'taking off' (cf 3:10, 12) indicates. It originally referred to clothing, and was no doubt suggested by the believer's unclothing before immersion and reclothing in new garments afterwards. Existentially, however, it is a long drawn-out process, and why this should be so is suggested by the qualities Paul ascribes to the two stages. Those of the 'old man' are essentially self-centred (3:5, 8), whereas those of the 'new man' are other-directed (3:12–16). A radical reorientation of the personality is involved.

It is tempting to think that by 'the new man' Paul means only what we do when we say that 'X is a new person', ie that a change for the better has taken place. This is certainly implied but the way 3:10–11 is formulated indicates that it does not exhaust his meaning. He says 'You have put on the new man . . . *where* there can be no distinction between Greek and Jew, . . .'. He is thinking in corporate terms, and the background is his presentation of the gospel in terms of 'the earthly man' (Adam) and 'the heavenly man' (Christ); cf 1 Cor 15:45–49. In these two figures Paul saw the two strands of our inheritance, an antithesis that he expresses elsewhere in terms of 'flesh' and 'spirit'. Adam is responsible for our being members of a community (the human race) distorted by sin. We are more than separate individuals; we are members of a wider whole that embraces the past as well as the present. We are influenced by the prevalence of sin all around us, and we have made our own contribution to its force. We thus bear a responsibility for the 'old man', who is at once ourselves and something wider. Christ is responsible for our being members of a new community in which humanity is restored to its pristine purity (read 3:10 against the background of Gen 1:26 f). It is as 'in Christ' that we are the 'new man'. In this perspective it is easy to see why the qualities of the 'new man' are other-directed. It is a question not merely of counteracting the basic selfishness of the 'old man', but of making the 'new man' progressively more actual, both in ourselves and in society. And Paul strongly underlines (3:17) that we should be grateful for what we have received (1:12), and for what we have been given the insight and capability to do.

The list of instructions (3:18–4:1) with regard to household duties had pagan prototypes. In Paul's presentation it is possible to detect a greater emphasis on the reciprocal nature of the duties, but the real innovation is in the motivation, 'because this pleases the Lord'. The same reality is viewed in a completely different perspective. What is done to the other is done to another (3:23). The service that is done to Christ is the actualisation of his presence in the world; it is to prolong his incarnation.

Having thus reduced to practical terms (for an immature community) the magnificent injunction of 3:14 ('And above all these put on love which binds everything together in perfect harmony') Paul turns to the problem of its relations with society in general (4:5–6). These verses should be compared with 1 Thess 4:11–12 and 1 Tim 3:7, because all three passages are devoid of any religious motivation. They reflect the sociological situation of the early church, which was that of a minority group in an environment which might turn hostile, and Paul's principal concern is to preserve harmonious relations. There is no suggestion of an organised apostolate by the church as such, but a community that lived as Paul desired it to live would have no need of words to leaven its environment.

1. Does the indicative, 'You have died' have any meaning if divorced from the imperative 'Put to death'? What relevance does this have to the theology of the sacraments?

2. Is it possible to be a christian without belonging to a christian community?

9

Personal news and final salutations
Col 4:7–18

Tychicus was probably the bearer of this letter as well as
of Ephesians (Eph 6:21) and Philemon. He is not mentioned in Philem, but the link is made by the assertion
that he will be accompanied by Onesimus, who was the
runaway slave of Philemon and the subject of the letter.
Tychicus will give the Colossians all the details about
Paul's condition. This reminds us that at this period a
letter was a comparatively rare means of communication,
and that in Paul's mind pastoral concern took very clear
precedence over personal affairs—at least in terms of
space! Mark seems to have been restored to Paul's good
graces, but some years before he had been the occasion
of a rather sharp difference of opinion between him and
Barnabas (cf Acts 14:36–39) which resulted in each
going his separate way. The other names are of less interest, save that of Luke, because it is this letter that
reveals to us that the author of the third gospel was
gentile (Paul finishes enumerating his Jewish friends in
4:11).

Paul had the custom of authenticating letters written
at his dictation (cf Rom 16:22) by adding a few words in
his own hand; cf 2 Thess 3:17, 1 Cor 16:21, Gal 6:11.

2 Thess 2:2 indicates quite clearly that forgery was not unknown. 'Remember my fetters' is not an appeal for sympathy, but for obedience to the gospel. He who is suffering for Christ has the right to speak on his behalf.

Philemon

Laurence Bright

Philemon

You can read Philemon in a couple of minutes. It is a personal letter, written from prison, about a slave called Onesimus, whom Paul is returning to his master. His name means 'useful', and this is what he has become to Paul (v 11). More important, he has become a christian, and the master is one too—pretty obviously they both owe their conversion to Paul (v 19). So Paul is asking for him back, and promising to make good any wrong he may have done (v 18). That's about all there is to it. Why was it preserved? What interest does it still have? Two answers are possible, if not highly plausible.

(1) This is the only purely personal letter from Paul's hand, and most scholars accept its authenticity. There has therefore been a good deal of speculation about the relationship between Paul and the other characters—Philemon, Apphia and Archippus as a family group, Onesimus their runaway slave, etc. Since there is no warrant in the text for such ideas, we need not linger over them.

But scholars (in most of whom there lurks an Hercule Poirot *manqué*) have also stepped in. There is a clear connection between this letter and Colossians: both Onesimus (Col 4:9) and Archippus (4:17) are mentioned, and there is an oddly long passage on slavery (Col 3:22–4:1). In his book *Philemon among the letters of Paul* (London 1960) John Knox suggests that Onesimus himself collected up the Pauline letters at a later date. This of course accounts for the inclusion of Philemon in the canon, whereas other such letters of equal unimportance have no doubt perished. Moreover, Onesimus may even be the author of Ephesians, so pauline in tone yet probably not a genuine Paul. An Onesimus (common name enough) was in fact bishop of Ephesus at the turn of the century. Knox also thinks that Archippus rather than Philemon owned the slave (his name comes last in v 1, but that may be to lead in to Paul's business with him), that he lived at Colossae, and that Philemon had to send the letter on to him from Laodicea. This clears up the second half of Col 4:16, 'the letter from Laodicea', leading into 4:17 and Archippus. We can leave the rest to Mr Eliot.

(2) More important is the matter of Paul's attitude to slavery (without generalising to that of the early church). Without too much conjecture, the connection with Colossians accounts for the length of the passage on slave-ethics among the other bits of conventional wisdom with which Paul closes that letter—the main subject of which is, after all, the high theology of Christ and the angelic powers.

But Paul on slavery is bound to stick in certain of our gullets. 'Slaves, obey your masters . . . Masters, treat your slaves justly' (Col 3:22–4:1). Clearly these ideas lie behind Philemon. There may be a hint in Phil 21 that Onesimus' freedom is being requested—but why can't Paul demand it openly? It seems to be enough that christian masters should behave more decently towards their slaves than the pagans did: there is no question, anywhere, of a change in social status. Apologists say that anything so revolutionary as a call for the general release

of slaves would have compromised the gospel's chances
of success. But this is nonsense. All that is or could be
immediately in question is emancipation within the comparatively small number of christian households. The
precedents are there in the Jewish law which required the
freeing of Jewish slaves every seven years (Ex 21 : 2; Deut
15 : 12–18) or at least at the jubilee (Lev 25). In Gal 3 : 28
Paul makes his great statement that in Christ Jesus there
is neither slave nor free: just what is it worth if it is to
have no actual consequence in the objective structure of
society?

*1. Is it legitimate to fasten on this letter, or similar
passages in others, to try and get a 'personal slant' on
Paul? Remember that a good deal that seems personal
(eg Rom 7 : 7–25 or much of Acts) is not really so—it is a
first-century convention of writing theology.*

*2. What of the scholarship that fastens on these things
for the purposes of the higher crossword puzzle?*

*3. What of the christian attitude to slavery? Was Paul
as politically conservative (though theologically radical)
as many a modern liberal christian? Why does it take so
long for christians to change the society they are a part of?*